VGM Opportunities Series

OPPORTUNITIES IN
PERFORMING ARTS CAREERS

Bonnie Bjorguine Bekken

Foreword by
Peter Hemmings
General Director
Los Angeles Opera

VGM Career Books
NTC/Contemporary Publishing Group

Library of Congress Cataloging-in-Publication Data

Bekken, Bonnie Bjorguine, 1941–
    Opportunities in performing arts / Bonnie Bjorguine Bekken ; foreword by
Peter Hemmings.—Rev. ed.
        p.   cm. — (VGM opportunities series)
    Includes bibliographical references.
    ISBN 0-658-00470-0 — ISBN 0-658-00471-9 (pbk.)
        1. Performing arts—Vocational guidance.   I. Title.   II. Series.

PN1580 .B45   2000
791'.023—dc21   00-39269

Published by VGM Career Books
A division of NTC/Contemporary Publishing Group, Inc.
4255 West Touhy Avenue, Lincolnwood (Chicago), Illinois 60712-1975 U.S.A.
Copyright © 2001 by NTC/Contemporary Publishing Group, Inc.
Printed in the United States of America
International Standard Book Numbers: 0-658-00470-0 (cloth)
                                                            0-658-00471-9 (paper)

01   02   03   04   05   06   LB   15   14   13   12   11   10   9   8   7   6   5   4   3   2

DEDICATION

In loving memory of my father, Odin M. Olson,
performing artist, beloved husband, cherished father,
idolized grandfather. Your grace belongs to the ages.

CONTENTS

ABOUT THE AUTHOR

Bonnie Bekken has been the editor of *Career World* and *Writing!* magazines, has taught in elementary and junior high schools, and currently is senior editor, specializing in guidance and career development materials, for Social Studies School Service in Los Angeles. She has written career columns for national syndication and won several awards from the Educational Press Association of America for excellence in educational journalism. Bonnie has been listed in *Who's Who of American Women* since 1989.

With capabilities in voice and violin, her earliest career aspirations were directed to the performing arts in general and musical theater in particular. A corresponding love for language lead her instead to education and writing—and the music of words.

FOREWORD

When I left university I had a classical degree and some experience as a performer, but no specific training for a career as an arts administrator. I learned on the job, bolstered by a passion for opera and the theater. This kind of career advancement does not happen anymore. Today, there are university courses in every conceivable aspect of arts administration, and I have taught many of them. Now, as I retire, I flatter myself that I can detect in students the qualities necessary for success. These qualities are application, the ability to effectively deal with a range of personalities, financial acumen, flexibility combined with a bit of stubbornness, and, above all, passion.

The role of the arts in society today is a vital one. People have more leisure time and they demand entertainment and stimulation. Opera, dance, theater, and cinema are active in large and small communities alike, and they all require proper managing. When I left university, everyone assumed that I would become a teacher. For some time, I avoided that career path, but now I find that I am a teacher and an educator—one who cultivates the talents that exist in young people. When I discover those who have drive and passion, I am encouraged about the future of the arts. *Opportunities in Performing Arts Careers* is an invaluable reference tool for just these types of people.

Peter Hemmings
General Director
Los Angeles Opera

PREFACE

I was told at an early age that I had talent: I performed, wrote poetry, made straight A's. I wanted to be an actress because I thought it would be fun. I would be rich and famous.

I quickly learned I was wrong. Acting was hard work, and talent wasn't enough. I took classes, joined a theater company, and earned a university degree in theater. Day in, day out, I studied. I performed—acting, dancing, "paying my dues." As an actress, I had to face rejection: not getting the role. My ego, my self-esteem, was hurt. Many times I grew frustrated and wanted to quit, but I was stubborn, and something deep down kept me going.

I finally had to take a good look at myself after turning down a $50,000-a-year job in public relations. Was I insane? Everyone else thought I was.

That's when I knew that the something deep inside me was love for what I did. I loved being who I was: a writer, a poet, a performing artist. So I set goals and was on my way.

I created a one-woman show, which is successful to this day; I started a film production company so I could write, direct, and produce my own projects. Love for what I do became my driving force—not fame, not money.

Today, as President of Hozhoni Productions, I bring Native American storytelling and art workshops into K–12 classrooms. This, along with my ongoing work as a consultant to studios, allows me to share knowledge with people who have decided to begin the climb up the mountain to become actors, writers, dancers, and musicians.

They will have to learn from their mistakes, as I did. They will have to learn to make peace with their pedestal, as I did. They will have to make their own journey, just as I did.

The path up the mountain is not easy, but perseverance and dedication will get you there. I wish you well on your journey. How you do it is up to you. Why you do it, where you will go—and when—all depend on that something deep inside that can keep you hanging on until you reach your goals.

Remember, if you can't make your dreams happen... who will?

Geraldine Keams
President of Hozhoni Productions

ACKNOWLEDGMENTS

Without the support and encouragement of Lawrence Alan, this book would not have been written.

I am indebted to Joyce Lain Kennedy, nationally syndicated careers columnist and forever friend, for her words of wisdom and for convincing me to take an assignment that proved to be vastly rewarding.

Special thanks go to Geraldine Keams, President of Hozhoni Productions. Both actress and educator, Ms. Keam's generosity of spirit and insightful contributions are cherished.

A debt of appreciation belongs to Dr. Kenneth B. Hoyt, distinguished professor at Kansas State University and former director of the United States Office of Career Education, for his comments and critique. I also wish to thank Dr. Darryl Laramore, author of *Careers* and coauthor, with Joyce Lain Kennedy, of *The Career Book.* Dr. Laramore is a leading light in guidance and career education—and one of the finest human beings I know.

Opportunities in Performing Arts Careers

Many have given their thoughts and their time. My thanks go to Denise Aguirre, Karen Mitchell, and Kay Roskam for their assistance in defining music therapy; Madelyn Berdes, my favorite "Phantom Dancer"; Mary Tokita and Michael Hackett, for their contributions to the UCLA Lab program and this book. The staffs and members of many associations in the arts deserve—and have—my appreciation for providing resources and suggestions. It is my wish that this book meet the expectations of all of you who assisted in its production, but, in the end, I hold the responsibility for its shortcomings. May you find them few.

INTRODUCTION

I feel the message of peace, the message of toler-
ance, the message of dialog, the message of nonvio-
lence, is very crucial and urgent. And if various
artists through their own professions promote human
values, that is very important.... Singers singing
songs reach a much larger audience [than I].

This observation on the power of musical performance
was made by Tenzin Gyatso, the Dalai Lama of Tibet, before his appearance at the 1999 World Festival of Sacred
Music in Los Angeles. The Dalai Lama called music "perhaps the most universal" of "the many forms in which human spirit has tried to express its innermost yearnings and
perceptions."

Whether your own career aspirations are for the theater,
dance, or a form of musical performance, the Dalai Lama's
words hold true: the performing arts are a translation of life
and a tribute to the endurance of the human spirit. But they
are more; they *are* life. In live performance, the artist can
touch the chords of human response in an audience. This

is a lofty realization, and one that carries a tremendous responsibility.

It's extraordinarily difficult to reach that plateau, to make a living in the performing arts. This book will show you what the possibilities are, if you have the talent and persistence to reach for them. Even if your performing artistry becomes an avocation rather than a source of livelihood, the Dalai Lama's message has merit.

Whatever your work, if it draws on the humanity in yourself and helps promote consideration and compassion in others, you have achieved the best of all possible things. You are a success.

Bonnie Bjorguine Bekken

CHAPTER 1

OPENING NIGHT:
MEDEA BY MOONLIGHT

The moon shines bright: in such a night as this...
Troilus methinks mounted the Troyan walls,
And sighed his soul toward the Grecian tents...
In such a night Medea gathered the enchanted herbs
That did renew old Aeson.

William Shakespeare, *The Merchant of Venice*

You are backstage of the open-air Greek amphitheater. A moist sea breeze and a backdrop of sun-bleached mountains remind you that this Mediterranean climate is ideal for the evening's opening night performance of Euripides' *Medea.* Your pre-performance jitters give way to an adrenalin surge as you peer out at the gathering crowd.

This is a new venue for you. And the year is—not 431 B.C.—but 2002. You are not in ancient Athens, but in modern-day Pacific Palisades, California, USA. You are at the extraordinary Getty Villa, where thespians and lovers of the ancient playwrights can experience Greek theater as it was when Euripides directed his first drama.

This newest and most endowed venue was once the Getty Museum. Built as a home for J. Paul Getty, the man never lived there, but locals and visitors enjoyed the art and antiquities collections housed in the Italian villa look-a-like perched on a cliff overlooking the Pacific. When the Getty Trust built a new museum, grand enough to properly display a growing collection, the original became "The Villa." Antiquities still are on display, but the special magic is the amphitheater—and you are there.

The big question is *why* are you there. It has taken you years to become a professional, to eke out a living as an actor. You've spent a king's ransom on schools and training. You've suffered through endless auditions and rejections. You've nurtured one of your most important assets, your body, denying yourself pleasures others take for granted.

A statistic: at any given moment during the past year, more than half of the 40,000 members of the Actors' Equity Association were out of work. They were unable to make a living in their career of choice. About 4,000 of those who found work reported performance earnings of less than $3,000 for the year. (Dancers and singers in musicals, as well as stage, motion picture, and commercial actors, can belong to Actors' Equity.)

As disappointing as the statistics may be, they don't tell the whole story.

WHY PERFORM?

For the dancer, a career is a short season, often concluding for the virtuosos of ballet by their midthirties. While most other workers are just reaching their stride, the dance for the dancer is over in this physically demanding field. Russian star Farukh ("King Farukh") Ruzimatov, at thirty-six, is able to substitute theatrical artistry for waning technical dynamics—and can still "wow" his audiences. He is a rare one.

For the musician, the season is longer, but so, too, is the road traveled. Robbie Robertson, of The Band, says he "had done eight years" on the road as a relative unknown, speaking as if touring were a kind of prison sentence: doing time while looking for the big break.

For the singer who would aspire to the opera stage, an intensive background in voice, acting, musicianship, dialect/language coaching, and music degrees may lead only to a role in the chorus—in itself a much sought-after position, despite grueling rehearsals. Jason Balla, tenor in the highly esteemed Lyric Opera chorus, tells of the strained voices he and other choristers endure by the end of the season.

For Janet Carley, who left Connecticut for Los Angeles with higher acting hopes, success is getting an audition call for a TV commercial.

What drives these artists—and perhaps you—to pursue a performing arts career despite the obvious drawbacks? Of course the applause, the recognition, is a symphony for self-esteem. But for the best—perhaps you—performing is a passion, an essential part of being. You perform because you must.

An astute student of human motivation, psychologist Abraham Maslow said, "A musician must make music... to be ultimately at peace with himself." Or herself, if you can forgive Mr. Maslow's slip from sex-fair language. Substitute "the dancer must dance" or "the singer must sing" or "the actor must act" to fit your personal dream. You already know it won't be easy. But there are ways to make it easier, and there may be performing options you haven't considered. That's what this book is about.

THE SCOPE: DANCERS, MUSICIANS, ACTORS

Music is a central part of many of the opportunities described in this book. You will investigate careers in opera: as singer, dancer, musician, conductor. You will explore opportunities as a musician: with orchestras, concert groups, and as a solo performer. You will appraise careers in dance, especially ballet and modern dance performance. Careers in popular music, in rock, and in jazz will also be discussed. You will identify opportunities in theater, in musical comedy, and will recognize the breadth of experiences in music video. A variety of careers in supportive professions, such as music education and music therapy, will be introduced to you. Would-be actors will probe theater, film, and television opportunities. And those who would like to consider unusual, nontraditional careers will find here off-beat opportunities to perform.

A Definition of Terms

Creative, dramatic expression. That three-word definition of the performing arts suggests a wide range of creative, dramatic ways to express yourself. Following is a list of occupations that are discussed, to greater or lesser degrees, in these pages.

Actor/Actress
Announcer
Autographer
Composer

Conductor
Dance Instructor
Dance Therapist
Dancer
Disc Jockey
Dramatic Coach
Educator
Film Director
Magician
Mime
Movement Notator
Music Director
Music Teacher
Music Therapist
Musician
Narrator
News Anchor
Pantomimist
Producer
Reconstructor
Singer
Storyteller
Therapist
Vocalist
Zoo-Performance Mime

PERFORMING ARTS CHECKLIST

There is no formula for success. There are, however, certain attributes and attitudes that contribute to success.
Do the criteria below fit you?

- The phrase "killing time" is foreign to you. You use time to create your future. You see an hour as more than an hour: you are, in each of its moments, creating a world. This knowledge makes you acutely conscious of your growth in your art.
- You have a realistic sense of the role of imagination. You can visualize yourself performing to a standing ovation, excelling in your art. This *imaging* (seeing yourself as a success) can help you define a goal and reach it. You recognize, though, that imaging also moves you away from the world of reality, beyond fact and experience, beyond cultivating performing skills, beyond the study, practice, planning, and hard work that will help you achieve an imaginative dream. Superior performers are more than dreamers.
- You have the ability to apply knowledge, to use what you know to make mental leaps in new circumstances. If an actor, you can use your understanding of history to interpret a character's response to the Black Death; if a dancer, your knowledge of physics contributes to your interpretation of a movement. You realize that

your art does not exist in a vacuum and that you bring all the facets of being to your performance.

- You know yourself. Seemingly a simple thing, self-knowledge is critical to career decision-making. In short, self-knowledge can be summed up by asking yourself this question: Which values do I want to protect in achieving my goal? With self-knowledge, you are able to work toward creating a world after your heart's desire; what does your heart desire? What is most valuable to you in life?

PASSIONS, PREFERENCES, AND PERSISTENCE

Whatever your personal performance preference, you already have identified a passion in yourself. It's why you have chosen to read this book. Performers—musicians, actors, dancers, singers—are those who have turned a passionate interest into a profession. Consider their persistence:

Nothing in the world can take the place of persistence. Talent will not; nothing is more common than unsuccessful men with talent. Genius will not; unrewarded genius is almost a proverb. Education will not; the world is full of educated derelicts.

Persistence and determination alone are omnipotent.

The words are attributed to Calvin Coolidge, but it is not likely that this American president of reputedly few words would have uttered so many. If he did, they were, perhaps, borrowed from a performer.

You've already been called a dreamer. But perhaps you're something else: a dreamer with determination. That's the stuff of which performers are made.

CHAPTER 2

MUSIC: UNDER STUDY

We are the music makers,
And we are the dreamers of dreams,
Wandering by lone sea breakers,
And sitting by desolate streams;
World-losers and world-forsakers,
On whom the pale moon gleams:
Yet we are the movers and shakers
Of the world forever, it seems.

Arthur William Edgar O'Shaughnessy,
Ode

A hush falls over the full house crowded comfortably into the cavernous theater at the Dorothy Chandler Pavilion in Los Angeles. This is the site of the Academy Awards, where the motion picture industry applauds its starts. Tonight there will be a different kind of applause for a different kind of performance.

Some will call it "operatic weirdness."

An opera, a work, will be staged. *Tancredi* is not part of the popular repertoire, but it's a grand old opera: the damsel in distress, the heroic soldier with distorted visions, polyphonic voices and stirring orchestrations—even tunes you can hum.

Tonight it will have something else: an understudy, Stephen Gould. Laryngitis has plagued the male lead for days. But Chris Merritt will go on. He will lip-synch his singing role, croak his way through the *recitatives,* opera's spoken narrative, rather than give up the stage to an understudy. Stephen Gould, although prepared to take center stage, will sing from the sidelines, clad in a business suit. He is a modern-day Invisible Man. He is there. You see him. But he is not a player.

Gould does not hold the heroine, nor does he wear Merritt's Crusades costume. But Stephen Gould is a crusader. He and many other talented young performers are a reality in the arts. Dedicated and persevering, these dancers and vocalists, instrumentalists and actors wait in the wings for the big break. While they wait, they work, perfecting their performance, sacrificing personal life for career.

THE SCOPE OF OPERA

Imagine a classified advertisement announcing openings for the following positions:

Conductor (one)—$200,000—$250,000, negotiable

Music Director (one)—$75,000 plus incentive benefits

Orchestral Section Leaders (sixteen)—$50,000 per season; $70,000 for concertmaster

Orchestral Section Members (seventy-five), all instruments—$30,000–$50,000 per season

Choral Director (one)—$40,000–$50,000, negotiable

Singers—$500 to $5,000 for principal roles requiring theatrical skill; $80 per performance for chorus members

Choreographer (one)—$5,000 per production

Dancers—above union scale, to $100 per performance

Supernumeraries (twenty) with superior dramatic and vocal abilities—$50 per performance

An unlikely ad, to be sure, given the nature of the hiring process in the arts, but the scope of performers in opera is a microcosm of the performance world. There is something for almost every talent. The very name, *opera,* with its Latin roots (oper, opus), connotes work.

All opera is divided into three parts: the dramatic (plot); the theatrical (costumes, sets, stage effects); and the musical (vocal, choral, instrumental). The purpose of this discussion is not to define what can—or cannot—be classified as opera, but rather to point out that there's more than one operatic avenue to achievement.

You're a serious performer. That does not mean you can aspire to only grand or traditional forms. Serious performers do not live exclusively in the domain of a standard reper-toire. Perhaps rock is your road. Does Pete Townshend (The Who) make a less valid statement in *Tommy* (Utopia is not attainable, and humans are too easily spiritually swayed) than the dramatic text of Gaetano Donizetti's *Lucia di Lammermoor* (A woman, forced into a loveless marriage, murders her husband and is doomed to insanity and a miserable death)? Does *Rent* demonstrate less concern with the human condition than *Otello*?

Like most good things, opera is evolutionary. The options for you to perform need not be limited to the 130 existing opera companies. You could be playing soon at a theater near you.

THE INSTRUMENTAL VOICE: OPERA SINGERS

> There is delight in singing, though none hear beside
> the singer.
>
> Walter Savage Landor,
> *To Robert Browning*

You have a voice—and you want to be heard. You are a soprano or a contralto, a tenor or a baritone, or a bass. You also possess a flair for the dramatic, a talent for the theatrical. You would *be* Tosca, *become* Rigoletto. Perhaps you have begun private vocal training. You are learning to care for your voice. You are learning technique. You will develop a repertoire. Your instrument is your voice.

You realize how important it is, too, to study languages, to become familiar with Italian, German, French, and Russian. You will perform in these, as well as in English. You will know the meaning of the words you sing, even if you do not fluently speak the language of the song.

The study of harmony and theory and the ability to sight-sing are goals, too. You are working on your intonation, your phrasing, and on vocal dynamics. You will sing no song before its time: You recognize that your voice needs to develop under careful direction.

Education and Training

The opera singer can afford to take time for a college degree; the degree can broaden general knowledge and enhance the ability to sing with self-assurance and act with understanding. Chances are, you will choose a school that offers the opportunity to participate in major opera workshops and solo recitals. There are many such schools, some public, some private, in which at least two opera productions are performed each year. The University of Illinois, Champaign-Urbana, produces six student operas; so does the Brevard Music Center in Brevard, North Carolina.

Chances are that you will look for a school that offers advanced opera or musical theater training.

JUILLIARD

The Juilliard has long set the standard for opera training. It offers a thirty-week, full-scholarship program with instruction in repertory coaching, diction, vocal training, acting, and movement. Auditions, given by appointment, favor the student with professional promise and one who is capable of taking on leading roles.

Only one out of every seven applicants is admitted to this ultraselective school, an acceptance rate that approximates that of Harvard and Princeton. Distinguished alumni include Leontyne Price and Itzhak Perlman.

OPERA APPRENTICESHIPS AND SUMMER PROGRAMS

Diva Marilyn Horne directs the summer voice program at the Music Academy of the West in Santa Barbara, California. The program, founded in 1947, offers classroom instruction, master classes, and considerable individual coaching. Horne says there are hundreds of applicants for each summer session, reflecting the growing popularity of opera in "a very visual age."

An innovative new program, Opera Overture, is held on campus at Pepperdine University in Malibu, California, and it is open to young voices: High school and undergraduate students are given the tools to start off on the right vocal track.

Other institutes offer summer sessions. The American Center for Music Theatre in Los Angeles, for example, has designed a six-week program with training in audition arias, art songs, monologues, scene study, movement, choreography, aerobics, improvisation, makeup, and languages. Limited financial assistance is offered. Trainees, who must audition for the program, are videotaped as a part of the learning experience.

More than a dozen American institutes offer such master classes. Some charge tuition, some do not. Advanced training, for a fee, also can be found in major operatic capitals in Europe.

THE CENTRAL OPERA SERVICE

The dynamics, the changes that characterize opera, offer a particular boon to the American singer. No longer are foreign performers fawned upon to the exclusion of their stateside counterparts. "The prejudice which favored only European stars (or Americans with European experience and, sometimes, new European names!) seems a thing of the past," says Beverly Sills in an introduction to *Career Guide for Young American Singers.*

The guide, published by the Central Opera Service (COS), offers a wealth of information to singers: sound suggestions for auditioning; a list of current grants; notice of regional, national, and international voice competitions held in the United States and Canada; and identification of selected foreign competitions open to American singers. The guide also contains addresses of opera and musical theater companies in the United States and Canada; a comprehensive list of tuition and nontuition institutes for advanced training, as well as a summary of colleges and universities that offer major workshops in opera; and a selected schedule of apprentice programs offering nonsinging opportunities in opera for accompanists, lighting designers, costumers, stage directors, musicians, libretto writers, and many other behind-the-scenes workers.

The *Career Guide* supplements the *COS Bulletin,* a quarterly publication that features news from opera companies, descriptions of new operas and companies, and updates on government and arts organizations. The bulletin is available to members. For membership and publication information, write to Central Opera Service, Metropolitan Opera Association, Lincoln Center, New York, NY 10023.

Financial and Personal Rewards

"My mother made all of her children feel that any dream was possible, that there was never a question but that we would achieve what we wanted," says Beverly Sills. If what you want is the security of a comfortable income, opera is not your kind of work.

Choristers, unsung heroes who sing, may have spent thousands of dollars on training, but their remuneration leaves something to be desired. Those in the Los Angeles Opera chorus who sing in all 56 yearly performances can earn about $18,000 to $20,000. Those in New York's Metropolitan Opera chorus earn from $80,000 to $115,000 for their much longer (220 performances) season. Choristers for Chicago's Lyric, working at all 80 performances, earn about half that. Earnings are less attractive at lesser venues: Recent U.S. Department of Labor studies report that most concert singers who are part of a chorus earn union minimum—$80 per performance. A soloist on the same stage may earn less than $300 per performance. There are, of course, the few who receive more than $25,000 for an appearance. Chances are, money was not the dream that drove them; in achieving a grander dream, money followed.

INSTRUMENTAL MUSICIANS

In Concert and Symphony

From old-guard to avant-garde, instrumental musicians most often find a niche—a specialty. Whether in orchestra or band, rock group or jazz combo, a career is much determined by the instrument (flute, cello, bassoon, guitar, piano, electronic synthesizer),

Most musicians with an eye on concert performance can expect to combine this activity with another occupation, which may or may not be music-related. Concert performance truly is music of the night, a reality that can allow the performer to earn a living elsewhere by day. Some travel; most live in cities, especially cities large enough to support concert activities.

Classical Acts

For instrumentalists with a classic persuasion, chairs may be found with one of the thirty major symphony groups in the United States, with regional orchestras, with the ninety-six metropolitan orchestras, or with hundreds of smaller groups. Musicians can work in opera, musical comedy, and ballet, with small chamber groups and (rarely) as soloists.

There is room for a well-known few to perform on television and radio, make recordings, and go on tour. The majority of concert musicians, though, are well-grounded in the home city of their orchestra.

On an average, the concert musician will make eight commutes to work each week. This includes rehearsals as well as performances. If the musician is with a major orchestra, the commute can be made for most of the year—from forty to fifty-two weeks. Small orchestras have shorter seasons. Except for musicians with large symphony orchestras, paid vacations and sick leave, hospitalization and life insurance, dental plans and bonuses are nearly unheard-of benefits. Some join the American Federation of Musicians, receiving benefits through union membership.

Status Equals Salary

Variations on the income theme are enormous with symphony orchestras: A musician can earn as little as $300 a week to more than $1,200. Those with status orchestras may earn more than $60,000 a year. The concert soloist may reap an average of $1,000 per appearance, according to the Music Educators National Conference, which reports that musicians with small ensembles can see earnings of anywhere from $50 to $5,000 for a performance.

It is possible to become a freelance member of an orchestra. Income will vary depending on the status of the orchestra and the geographic region. Local unions set rates. Musicians may earn more than $90 for a performance and about half that for each rehearsal. Musicians associated with a university or institute usually earn modest salaries, but they receive tenure and a pension. Musicians with armed forces orchestras earn base pay.

Education

Hundreds of colleges, universities, and music conservatories offer degree programs in music. Should the serious student of music sign up? A degree is not required. Equivalent training is. Extensive and ongoing musical experience is essential to acquire playing skill, fluency in sight-reading, skill in transposing and improvising, and familiarity with the instrumental literature. These can be realized in a number of ways:

- private study with an accomplished teacher
- practice with an accomplished group
- attendance at music camps
- enrollment in a college or university program or a music conservatory

College and conservatory study usually calls for a qualifying audition. An audition also is required by some music camps. The rigor of these requirements helps the musician prepare for the rigors of the job search.

Formal education also provides the music student with the opportunity to investigate creative performing options.

In short, the more you know about what you can do with instrumental talent, the more likely you are to find your niche and to be able to support yourself in music. A degree in music education, for example, can lead to satisfying work during the day—and still allow the talented to play their music at night.

COMPOSITION 101

You have performing talent. Perhaps you're a gifted keyboardist. You can, and do, perform. But you're driven by another desire. You want to compose, to write the music that becomes part of the repertoire. Someday, they'll be playing your song or performing your opera or dancing to your score.

On the surface, achieving the dream is as simple as A, B, C:

A. Write great music.
B. Learn the business end of music, including program plans for orchestras, so you know which orchestras perform what kinds of music—and how they budget.
C. Meet conductors.

Under the surface, however, pokes a sharp reality: As a composer, you are competing with the likes of Beethoven, Bach, and Brahms. You're waging a battle against tradition. It's a battle, nevertheless, worth engaging in, for music is a dynamic, living thing. Was Beethoven diminished because Bach was born first?

Women in Composition

"The first thing new composers must do is dream—because your dreams are the condition for being able to make a living in music."

So says Tania Maria, jazz composer (*The Lady from Brazil*), who began marching to the beat of her own keyboard when she was twelve. If composing is your dream, and you realize the tremendous odds against earning a living through composition, you've already decided to test yourself. Will you succeed?

Music knows no gender. The term "woman composer," however, is practically an *oxymoron*—a contradiction. Rare is the symphonic composition attributed to a female, although women in composition are hardly news. Nadia Boulanger taught harmony to Aaron Copland. Vivian Fine moved from keyboard to composer of symphonies, music for ballet, and opera.

"I've probably been composing since I was eight or nine years old," Frances White, a doctoral candidate at Princeton, reports. But she never thought her love for, and talent in, composition could become a career option until she was in high school. "As a little kid, I didn't think that was something that women did. All the composers I knew about were men," she told interviewers for *Peterson's Professional Degree Programs in the Visual & Performing Arts: 2000*. Her most recent composition was commissioned by a French electronic music studio, and it will premier at an international festival.

Beyond the ABC's

Whatever your gender, success in composition is hard work. But somebody has to do it. If that's you, here are some basics beyond the ABC's:

- Develop superior musicianship, superior diplomacy (people skills), superior sales skills (to sell your composition), and, preferably, superior education. (A graduate degree in music is not a requirement, but conservatory training can make sense. Any opportunities you can find to be around other composers can help.)

• Attend workshops and seminars whenever you can. The American Society of Composers and Publishers (ASCAP) offers these learning opportunities, as do other organizations.

• If possible, attend an arts program in a public education setting or at a private academy of arts. A student who majors in composition at the Interlochen (Michigan) Center for the Arts, for example, can begin college-level theory courses in music while in high school. He or she will spend at least two hours a day composing concert art (so-called "classical") music. Student compositions are performed in school concerts. An entrance examination in knowledge of music and ear training, as well as private auditions, is required.

Summer music camps offer another opportunity to learn and practice composition. Composition majors at Interlochen's National Music Camp devote most of their time to producing original music to be performed on campus. Appel Farm Arts and Music Center in Elmer, New Jersey, offers a less structured summer program in the arts. If you are considering a summer music camp, talk to students who have already participated in a program to find out if it will provide the kind of experience you seek.

Composing Commissions

The income a composer makes is usually based on commissions or royalties or performance rights fees. If you are commissioned to write a work, your earnings can vary, depending on who hires you. Royalties pay pennies for each sale of a music recording. Composers also can sell the right to perform a work. This fee varies.

A very few composers, such as Libby Larsen of the Minnesota Orchestra, are employed to compose. Most composers perform, teach, or work in some other way to earn a living.

DANCING WITH DANGER: THE CONDUCTOR

"I very much like the danger of the theater," says Randall Behr, speaking of the complexities of conducting opera. The danger is there, too, in simply going after a career as a conductor: There are virtually no positions available. Still, for those with the temperament and talent, it's a delicious danger.

Before he conducted the Strauss opera *Salome,* Randall Behr spent two years in close study of the score. Intensive study is a given in conducting an orchestra. But that barely scratches the surface of the conductor's job demands. Because conducting is so visible, because it takes the performer to major cultural centers, because it seems to epitomize glamour, the hard work conducting requires is too easily overlooked.

Conductors do more than lead orchestras. They audition musicians and select them; they direct rehearsals. Conductors choose the orchestra's repertoire, planning for an entire season. They spend untold hours studying scores to authentically re-create a composer's intent. They also assume responsibility for staging, for acoustics. Conductors are called on to help raise funds to support the orchestra. In addition to orchestral duties, they make numerous public appearances, leaving little time for personal life.

All this for a salary as slim as $10,000 a year. There are the few who can command salaries in the $300,000 range, those who, like the already legendary Riccardo Muti, divide time between a great orchestra (the Philadelphia) and a great opera company (La Scala). Most, however, divide time between conducting an orchestra and conducting classes: They teach at a university or at seminars. Some may be music directors for one orchestra and conductors for another. Others hold a steady position with one orchestra and conduct at other venues when opportunity knocks.

A Crusader for Latin American Composers

For six years, Gisele Ben-Dor has conducted the Santa Barbara Symphony during the winter—commuting from her home in New Jersey. From time to time, she has led the New York Philharmonic. She also was conductor for the Boston Pro Arte Chamber Orchestra.

Wherever she may be, Ben-Dor brings drive and devotion to her assignment. In Santa Barbara, she has made it her mission to bring Latin American composers to light. Early in the year 2000 she planned and executed a four-day Silvestre Revueltas festival—an exercise in education and awareness for a composer she believes has been ignored and unfairly described as "difficult."

Her crusade for Revueltas has its roots in her childhood. At age twelve, she organized her friends in Montevideo, Uruguay, into a band—and became the leader.

"I had no idea it could be a profession or that I would someday be doing this as a living," she told Josef Woodard, writer for the *Los Angeles Times Calendar.* She learned music—both classical and "street." "As a kid, I played a lot of Latin American folk music."

Ben-Dor credits her passion in large part to the late Leonard Bernstein, who recognized her talent in 1982 and brought her to the Tanglewood Young Artists Orchestra. She spoke of Bernstein's devotion to music, his fire: "That fire is what keeps you going. It's treacherous, it's bumpy. Working with Bernstein was like a light along the way."

Education

A conservatory or college degree, though not required, is of growing importance to those who want to become conductors. Certainly a conductor will have equivalent training through seminars, private study, and "ladder experiences": conducting chamber ensembles, school orchestras or youth bands, and community orchestras. Many conductors have been instrumental members of an orchestra. They play at least one, probably several, instruments. They are familiar with at least one, probably several, foreign languages.

Summer learning experiences, such as the Tanglewood, Massachusetts, seminars, can be important opportunities, not only to develop conducting style and skills, but to develop musical contacts—and, perhaps, a relationship with an experienced mentor, someone who can guide the young conductor in acquiring style and skills.

The image of the charismatic conductor, one with remarkable stage presence, is a cliché. But, like most clichés, it has its roots in truth. Conductors perform. Theirs is a theatrical artistry.

CHAPTER 3

MUSIC: JAZZ, ROCK, BLUES, POP

> I think the only way that people will ever be able to see a picture of unity is through music, through dance and rhythms coming together.
>
> Stevie Wonder, in *Rolling Stone*

It's rock-hard work, breaking into the contemporary music scene—but somebody's got to do it. Marcus Roberts did.

Roberts lost his eyesight as a child. Two cataract operations left him with only the perception of light. He began piano lessons. After nine years of classical studies, Roberts entered a contest at the Jazz Educators' Convention in Chicago. He won. That was 1982. Roberts joined the Wynton Marsalis group shortly thereafter. Eight years later, his solo debut album, *The Truth Is Spoken Here,* was number one on the *Billboard* jazz chart. His vast knowledge of the jazz

canon served him well during his 1994 tour as music director for the Lincoln Center Jazz Orchestra—shortly after his
thirtieth birthday.

JAZZ: THE PERFORMER'S MEDIUM

Perhaps more than any other musical form, jazz is a performer's art. The melody in a performance is of less importance than what the performer does with the melody. The
jazz musician, or vocalist, improvises on the melody.

A career in jazz is not so likely to be improvised. Marcus
Roberts's classical training gave him the groundwork on
which to make his own music. Background in classical music is not essential, of course. Jazz takes many forms,
boasts performers with widely varying experiences. In
some forms, a background drenched in orthodox, classical
music is a negative.

As for all professional musicians, the jazz musicians will
have started early, looked for opportunities to perform, and
have spent years practicing to gain skill, knowledge, and
the performing artistry needed to interpret music.

Training through private study, with a group, and at a
conservatory (preferably all three) is typical. For conservatory study, expect to audition. A growing number of jazz
musicians and vocalists attend a college or university

where they may study music theory and analysis. Most important, the jazz musician needs an education in the principles that underlie all music, regardless of period or style. This can be learned in—or outside of—a formal setting.

Some jazz musicians belong to support groups that can be instrumental to personal growth, such as the AACM (Association for the Advancement of Creative Musicians) or BAG (Black Artists Group).

Downbeats

Jazz musicians perform under difficult circumstances—in smoky clubs, on long road tours. Stamina, as well as talent, is needed—as is optimism. Club dates can be hard to get, and club audiences can be rudely unaware of a performance. Jazz musicians play for pay when others are playing for fun, in the evenings and on weekends.

Work is centered in cities where audiences are large enough to support performances. For the jazz musician, these include New York, Chicago, New Orleans, and St. Louis—cities with a strong jazz tradition. Even in centers such as these, the audience for jazz can be disappointing. Chicago, for example, has a wealthy history in blues/jazz evolution and is a city that has produced its own jazz style. Yet many of its finest performers found recognition only after establishing themselves in New York. Sadly, New

York clubs also don't have enough work for everyone. Jazz musicians enter the field knowing how slim the chances are for success.

Changing Patterns

The field itself is expanding, not in demand for performers, but in other ways. First, changes and growth in jazz make the metamorphosis of a butterfly look static. Also, many jazz musicians are combining jazz with other musical forms—in search of an audience. Jazz fusion is a case in point. And there are other, unexpected musical fusions.

Ornette Coleman is a jazz veteran of more than forty years. His biggest commercial success came in 1988 when he and his group, Prime Time, recorded *Virgin Beauty*. It made the second spot on *Billboard*'s jazz chart. It sold more in its first year of release than anything Coleman had done in the past. And it featured, on three tracks, a guitarist named Jerry Garcia, of the Grateful Dead. It could be that some of those sales came from Grateful Dead fans.

POP, ROCK, AND RAP

Who else is making news in music? Andy Prieboy, whose rock career was dead, turned to writing a musical,

White Trash Wins Lotto, which drew sellout audiences in Los Angeles's Roxy Theater after its 1999 open. The satirical musical, inspired by the life of Axl Rose of Guns N' Roses, has become one of the most talked about rock sendups since *This Is Spinal Tap.* When his last rock recording, *Sins of Our Fathers,* went nowhere in 1995, he could have stuck it out playing poorly attended gigs in small clubs. Instead he turned to sweetly melodic satire. The lesson he learned: When you're failing in your chosen profession, try to remember why you chose it in the first place.

Something new. If you've got it, and if you can get the right people to recognize it, a performing career—or at least a performing year or two—can be had.

Pay to Play: RAPP

On the other hand, the performer can be had. It's becoming commonplace for young musicians to pay a club for a chance to prove themselves in performance. An association of performers that calls itself RAPP (Rockers Against Pay to Play) regularly pickets California clubs where acts must purchase as much as $1,200 worth of admission tickets before they are booked. With the stiff competition in the music business, many struggling musicians are willing to come up with the money. It's a buyer's market.

Club Dates

Those performers of popular forms who sing or play an instrument well can find opportunities, if not stardom, through club dates. Not the pay-for-play variety, *club dates* is a term that refers to playing the party circuit: weddings, birthdays, graduations, school events. The site may be indoors or out. You could perform for people who think you should be a recording star—or for people who won't even listen to you. You could, if playing alfresco, battle bugs, wind, rain, and humidity on an outdoor stage. And you could, if people buy your style, move on to become a concert artist or find studio opportunities.

Machine *vs.* Musician

One of the commodities being bought is technology. Recording-studio sounds and high-energy entertainment are pushing rap ahead, leaving rhythm and blues behind, without the dusty, quieter drama of the R&B great voices of the past: Sam Cooke, Aretha Franklin, Otis Redding. Audiences aren't buying great voices and quiet drama. Says Jerry Wexler, a record producer who worked with Franklin: "If Otis Redding came along today, he might not even get a contract. Some record company executive might tell him,

'You sing too strong, kid. You sing too good. You'll never make it.' "

"Styles change," Wexler told Dennis Hunt of the *Los Angeles Times.*

Studio opportunities with recording companies usually pay more than $60 an hour. Earnings are about the same in motion picture (*session*) recording. The problem, of course, is in putting enough hours back-to-back to earn a living. Today, much studio recording is being done with electronics: machines rather than musicians.

In an already wickedly competitive marketplace, musicians face an economic reality: The traditional worker versus technology. The huddled masses of musicians and their supporters who picketed clubs a decade ago are not unlike employees in the manufacturing sector who went on strike when technology threatened their livelihood.

Displaced workers, whether in manufacturing or music, do have choices: They can look elsewhere for work—or they can retrain to redirect their careers.

Technology won't go away.

THE MUSIC/TECHNOLOGY MIX

In her nationally syndicated careers column, Joyce Lain Kennedy describes one way of overcoming technological barriers. For students of music who also have electronic/engineering aptitude, Kennedy suggests a career where music is the product, and technology is how it's made.

Music engineering technology, because it is a new discipline, is offered at few universities. Two colleges, Miami University in Coral Gables, Florida, and Ball State University in Muncie, Indiana, have degree programs that can lead to a unique career—as an engineering consultant for a music company, for example. Says Kennedy: "There's a lot of babble about computer music not replacing live musicians, but it does and will. [Music engineering technology] is a classic case of joining what you can't beat."

The electronics movement was still in its infancy as the new century was born. This is because it has yet to unite with the single most important element in popular music: the song. Nothing touches us as deeply as a great song.

Robert Hillburn, pop music critic for the *Los Angeles Times,* expressed it most eloquently. "Whatever form pop music takes in the coming years, someone will eventually step forward to express our desires and doubts in a way that will define that age. That artist may be holding a guitar or standing beside a synthesizer, but it's the song that will connect with a generation—and anyone else who is willing to listen."

CAREERS FOR SINGERS

For those popular musicians whose instrument is their voice, but who do not aspire to the theater/opera, here is a handful of possibilities:

1. Let's take it from the top. A concert soloist can earn form $350 a performance to sky's-the-limit income. Employment opportunities: next to nothing.
2. Can heaven help you? A church choir soloist earns from $30 to more than $500 for each performance and may also be paid for rehearsal time. Performance dates, of course, are infrequent.
3. Want to be part of a bigger picture? Community choral groups usually are volunteer opportunities. Singers participate for the fun and experience. However, some groups do pay minimal performance fees, from $200 to a few thousand dollars a year.
4. Join the club. As a singer for a nightclub and/or with a dance band, average earnings are about $225 a week.
5. Go for video. As part of a vocal group for network television shows, singers can draw a minimum of $125 per performance. For local television, rates run about $75 per show.

Gross Income

The Rock-Star-Formerly-Known-As-Prince earns an estimated $36 million a year. Tantalizing incomes like this can attract young singers who are convinced they are just as good—or better—vocalists. But it can be a fatal attraction. Instead of multimillion dollar contracts, the vocal majority belong to the sing-for-your-supper category of earnings. If money is not the object, singing engagements can be a lark; rarely are they a living.

DISC OR VIDEO JOCKEY

It may not be your own music, but you can play it as a disc jockey or video jockey. It's not unusual for the DJ or VJ to come from a musical background. Knowledge of music in general and of a musical genre in particular is important at some stations. Beyond that, a necessary element for the business is a distinctive style, an on-air personality that will win listeners.

Other than "a voice and a rap," a disc jockey may be required to demonstrate onstage ability, to promote the station by making appearances at record stores or charitable events, for example. Many deejays add club host or concert host to their list of job duties.

Hours can be a rude awakening: midnight to five in the morning, six A.M. to ten A.M. In fact, top performers for a station will draw the latter slot—the morning "drive time."

At smaller stations, a disc jockey may play the role of music director or program director. The physical act of playing the recordings and handling the sound controls also falls to deejays with small stations. The basic job description, though, calls for the jock to introduce recordings, commercials, news, and public announcements—and to do it with flair: the better the ability to ad lib, the bigger the audience.

Many disc jockeys earn a following because they really know jazz, rock, country, or classical music, and their opinions are respected.

Openings for beginners are scarce, and some pay pennies or less. The newcomer can break in as a student intern, without pay, doing fill-in airtime and acting as resident gofer while proving a broadcasting talent. Expect to start with a small station in a small community, where salaries sometimes are barely above minimum wage. Bigger incomes, up to and more than $150,000 a year, come with experience, a following, and in major markets, such as Chicago, New York, or Los Angeles. Major markets are generally even more difficult to break into.

Training and Trade Schools

A degree is not required, but courses in communications and broadcasting through college or vocational-technical programs can enhance the chance to find work. Consider college, too, for broader knowledge and, possibly, the opportunity to work on the college station.

Be wary of private vocational schools. Some trade schools promise attractive, "make-you-a-star" broadcasting programs. In reality, the school's intent may be only to make money for the owner. Not all trade schools are disreputable, but no one wants to invest money and time in a bad apple. Check the school's credentials through your state department of consumer affairs or the attorney general's office. Also, make the school prove its reputation. Ask for names of graduates. Find out what percentage have a job in the industry. And talk with students and grads.

Let the starry-eyed beware.

PROMOTING YOURSELF

Breaking into contemporary music is difficult, but you're determined to do it in spite of the odds. You have the minimum entry-level requirement: talent. Take it to the people who buy it: record companies, agents, managers. Would-be deejays should approach radio stations.

You'll need to make a demo CD that sells you at your best. The demo must be of the highest quality. If you know sound recording and can use good equipment, you can make your own demo; otherwise, look for a good price from a commercial sound studio. Or (depending on whether the visible you is as important as the sound you make), put together a videotape demo. The music company executives you send your demos to will take them at face value: The demo *is* you. Don't waste your time and money sending them anything but your top performance. Follow up each mailing with a letter and/or phone call.

Expect rejections. Almost all performers who went on to make a sale first suffered rejection.

While you're keeping the post office busy, keep looking for opportunities to show your stuff at clubs. You may play for pay, pay to play, or perform without pay. Whatever the financial arrangement, it's a chance to be seen and heard. If you live in a community where records are produced, seek out playing engagements at places that showcase talent and are frequented by agents and record-company talent seekers.

A suggestion: Before you send your demo, call the record company. Ask for a contact name—the A&R (artist and repertoire) department head. In some cases, this may be the owner. Larger companies hire A&R executives. Address this contact directly in the cover letter you send with your demo. Names are important.

There's another good reason to establish personal contacts: If your demos are rejected repeatedly, you just might want to consider another career in music, other than performing. There may be a way you can work behind the scenes—for a recording company, for example.

Heads-Up Performance

And keep your chin up. If you took a cross section of the Alps—a rugged, peaks-and-valleys profile—you'd get a visual image of a career path in popular music. You can go up, and you can go down. When your career hits a crevice, renew your efforts and look for other performing opportunities—or look for another career. Rejection doesn't need to be failure; it can lead to breakthrough thinking, redoubled efforts, and success.

CHAPTER 4

MUSIC AND DANCE:
EDUCATORS AND THERAPISTS

Music must take rank as the highest of the fine arts—
as the one which, more than any other, ministers to
human welfare.

Herbert Spencer,
On the Origin and Function of Music

Superior performance is not limited to the stage. Those who *can,* teach. Those who are capable tutor tomorrow's musicians. Those who are able may turn musical talent to musical service through a career in music therapy.

Educators and therapists hold a special distinction in the realm of music: They are qualified for a career in their chosen discipline, and they can also, if they choose, perform professionally as musicians. Further, both educators and therapists are looking at an upbeat market for their skills and talents.

If you have people skills as well as musical ability and are willing to invest the time in a degree—preferably two—consider these careers.

TEACHING BY SEMESTER

On a scale of one to five, where do instrumental music teachers rank among educators? A perfect three. Supply and demand are in balance, based on a study conducted annually for ASCUS (Association of School, College, and University Staffing) by James Atkin, Kansas State University, who examines all areas of elementary and high school education.

The largest number of full-time positions for music educators can be found in the nation's public and private schools. Teaching in a public school can be very different from teaching in a private school or studio. The emphasis is on music appreciation in the public schools—rather than on participation.

The music teacher at the preschool and K–6 (kindergarten through sixth grade) levels will teach and lead classes in singing, music appreciation, movement and dance, playing instruments, and, sometimes, music composition as well.

Educators in middle, junior high, and senior high schools teach and lead students in choral and instrumental groups and musical theater productions. At the secondary level, the music instructor may teach courses in music history, theory, and related arts.

Education and Earnings

Public school instructors will have a teaching certificate as well as at least a bachelor's degree and a broad background in music. They need performing skill, of course, in either voice or an instrument.

Salary varies, depending on geographic location, from approximately $20,000 to $50,000 annually, according to the Music Educators National Conference. Some districts pay more to experienced teachers. In Anchorage, Alaska, for example, teachers can top $50,000 a year, indicate studies conducted by the National Education Association.

To supplement teaching income, the public school educator may work with community music or recreation groups. Some conduct choirs.

IN STUDIOS

A studio can refer to any one of many settings for the private teacher. It may be a corporate music school, such as the Yamaha Music Program, which introduces very young children to the keyboard. The setting may be a music store in a suburban mall or a city office building. Or it can be the teacher's own home or the home of a student.

Teachers who work out of home are self-employed. Other studio teachers work under a business relationship with the store or school and may be either salaried or work freelance, setting their own hourly rates. In either case, earnings may range from $5 for a lesson to more than $75. The studio teacher does not need a college degree, but will have substantial skill in the instrument.

For the studio teacher, there is no such thing as a paid sick day or vacation. Health insurance and other benefits also do not come with the territory for the self-employed. On the other hand, the studio teacher can screen students and has the option of creating a work schedule with more flexibility than that of the public school teacher.

AT THE COLLEGE/CONSERVATORY

It's not unusual for a college to recruit a successful performing artist to join the faculty. In situations such as this, the educator may have gained entry with a master's degree or, in a few, rare cases, without any degree. Generally speaking, however, teaching at the university level demands a doctorate, as well as performance skill in at least one instrument.

Educators at postsecondary institutions specialize in one or two areas, such as music history and literature, music education, musicology, performance, electronic music, composition, conducting, music theory, or music therapy. They may conduct choruses and orchestras and coach chamber music groups.

Serious Business

For those who love performing and working with performers, teaching at the college and conservatory level can be deeply satisfying. Educators in these schools work with serious students of music who want to learn all they can while in school. This also places a burden of proof on the educator, who must study continually to be able to satisfy the most talented students' demands.

Teachers in a college setting may be required to conduct research and produce papers for publication in their area of specialization. In some schools, "publish or perish" applies to the music department as well as to other academic fields. Being published helps promote the educator within the school system—from assistant or associate professor to full professor.

Employment and Earnings

Earnings depend on the reputation of the school and its location, as well as the professional status of the music educator. Most educators will have teaching experience before they win an appointment to a college or conservatory staff. Salaries for the beginning assistant professor can start as low as $18,000 a year. Associate professors may earn incomes ranging up to $30,000. A professor may earn less than that at a small college and twice that figure at a more prestigious institution.

A willingness to relocate can help the student of music get a first position with a college or conservatory. Nevertheless, the employment outlook for college teaching in general—and music in particular—is only fair. The best teachers are inspiring teachers. The job market for postsecondary music education, though, is anything but inspiring.

SUPERVISION IN MUSIC

In contrast to the college or conservatory teacher, who must enjoy performing or working with performers, is the music supervisor. Charged with administrative tasks, the music supervisor will have a background, and a bachelor's degree, in music, plus a graduate degree in supervision and administration.

Supervisors are hired for individual schools, at the district level, and by the state. All positions call for directing activities of teachers in music education, planning and developing the music education curriculum, and meeting with parents, other educators, board members, and administrators. The supervisor may be responsible for ordering equipment and materials for music programs. Although some music supervisors have opportunities to work directly with students, this is a field far closer to paper-chasing than to performance.

Supervisors' salaries start at about $18,000 annually. At district and state levels, earnings range up to and more than $50,000 a year.

GUIDING LIGHTS: DANCE EDUCATORS

Training is everything. The peach was once a bitter almond; cauliflower is nothing but cabbage with a college education.

Mark Twain,
Adventures of Huckleberry Finn

Beatriz Rodriguez saw a dance production of *Sleeping Beauty* when she was eight years old. She was enchanted.

Today Rodriguez is captivating kids, much as she, herself, was once enthralled. She appears in a video version of the classic ballet *Billy the Kid,* which is used in classrooms to bring performing arts to the schools. Rodriguez also appears live in special performances of the Eugene Loring ballet, performances held just for fifth-graders. Sponsored by the Los Angeles Music Center Education Division in collaboration with the Blue Ribbon Children's Festival, the program is a study in both dance appreciation and student motivation.

Though Rodriguez has strong ties to education, she is not a dance teacher. She has, however, qualities and skills that are basic to teaching dance:

- the ability to inspire
- a philosophical understanding of dance and education
- a desire to help others learn
- good mental and physical health
- knowledge of many forms of dance
- knowledge of music, lighting, costuming
- personal talent

Those Who Can...Teach Dance

Not every dancer is capable of being a dance instructor. Beatriz Rodriguez has many of the necessary qualities and could well turn her attention to creating peaches from bitter almonds. But there is more to teaching dance. Dance teachers have special skills and knowledge:

- anatomical understanding of how the body works
- the ability to relate well to people
- the ability to choreograph dances
- patience and perseverance
- administrative ability

Rodriguez also has the background to become a dance teacher in a studio setting: performance experience. Performance experience can be substituted for college degrees to qualify a dancer to teach in some conservatory settings.

Where to Teach

Beyond studio and conservatory settings, would-be dance teachers can apply their art in day-care settings, adult education programs, public schools, colleges or universities, special education programs, and drama schools.

Training varies for these settings. Some dancers can find work with children in day care without a bachelor's degree—although a degree is preferred. Public school dance teachers must have at least a bachelor's degree in dance. College and university dance teachers need a master's degree in dance and/or performance experience. Most conservatories also look for teachers with graduate degrees in dance and/or performing experience.

Another avenue opened for dance instruction when Americans developed a fascination with fitness. It is not unusual to find dance teachers working in fitness clubs, physical arts/recreation centers, and even in church basements. Students may be children; more likely they will be adults interested in using ballet, modern dance, jazz, or aerobic routines to enhance their well-being.

Salary Schedules

Earnings vary wildly. The dance teacher in a public school or college setting may earn from $22,000 to $45,000 a year. Studio teachers average from less than $10,000 a year to more than $40,000.

Dancers who begin their own studios can expect to struggle to stay afloat financially while they build the business. One dancing couple who decided to open their own studio continue to juggle the budget after several years. Both had danced professionally. Both love the dance and teaching. But neither can teach full-time. Scheduling, keeping track of money matters, hiring (and firing) pianists, and promoting the studio all take their toll on the couple's time.

Nevertheless, they are happy. Dance always has been the focal point of their lives. Teaching dance keeps it that way.

MUSIC THERAPY

Changes. Those who like to make them may be well-suited to a career in music therapy. At its core, music therapy is about change, bringing about desirable change in behaviors and abilities.

Music therapists work to restore and improve mental and physical health for clients of all ages. Many music therapists work in schools with children who are learning disabled or physically disabled, emotionally disturbed, or culturally disadvantaged.

Therapists also work with adults, including geriatric patients. Settings include hospitals, clinics, community mental health facilities, and special service agencies.

Some registered music therapists work in their own studios with children and/or adults referred by psychiatrists and other health professionals.

Models and Modes

Given the audience they serve, those who perform in music therapy must be emotionally stable and have stamina. The therapist serves as a role model, with music as the mode. According to the National Association for Music Therapy (NAMT), patience, tact, understanding, and a healthy sense of humor are indispensable qualifications, as are imagination, creativity, and the ability to work closely with others—both patients and personnel in therapeutic groups.

Education and Training

Training for this specialty is unique: It combines a music curriculum with extensive study of behavioral and biological sciences. The bachelor's degree in music therapy, says the NAMT, "prepares for intelligent living and understanding because it does not stop with the introspective perfection of musical performance." Courses cover theory and practice of music therapy, psychology, sociology, and anthropology. Music courses make up about half of the music therapy curriculum.

Beyond campus work, the student of music therapy completes six months of clinical training—an *internship*—in an approved program under the direction of a registered music therapist. This is the equivalent of practice teaching for certification in education.

Openings and Salary Schedules

Positions for therapists exist in almost every community, and the chances of finding one are optimistic. Salaries can

range dramatically, depending on location. Annual earnings start at about $20,000 and plateau at about $40,000.
It's not for everyone who wants music in a career setting.
As is true for teaching, music therapy can be frustrating
and the kind of work that is difficult to leave when the
workday ends. The would-be therapist would be wise to
spend volunteer or paid time in a rehabilitation setting before going after a degree.

Denise Aguirre: Happiest when Helping

If music therapy hadn't existed, Denise Aguirre would
have invented it. The field was made to order for her.

When she began college, Denise was a theater major.
Among her many qualifications, she has an excellent singing voice and an energy and exuberance that come through
loud and clear when she speaks.

And Denise loves to perform. She had thought about a
performing career for a long time. But as her undergraduate days progressed, Denise, intelligent and with an unusu-
ally high degree of self-knowledge, became aware of
aspects that would alter her life.

First: "I knew I didn't want to live day-to-day waiting for
a role." Denise saw friends in just that predicament. With
abilities in acting and music, they had graduated and gone
on to "do things that had nothing to do with music," just to
earn a living.

Second: "I'm the sort of person who is happiest when I'm helping someone."

"If only," Denise Aguirre thought, "there was some way to use music and help people at the same time."

When a speaker visited the college campus to describe music therapy, Denise was elated. She had found it—the best of both worlds.

SATISFACTIONS

What was her most satisfying experience during her college days doing field work?

> There are so many that I get excited when I think about them. Just this semester I worked with one- to three-year-olds with Down's syndrome. One child would not hold on to a mallet to play a drum. He would put the mallet in his mouth. I worked with him one on one, without success, for three weeks.
>
> Then—he did it! He hit the drum! He only did it twice, but he did it. I was bouncing; I was so excited.
>
> If you tell people who are not in music therapy that 'so and so smiled today in my session,' they wonder how you can get so enthusiastic about such a little thing. But if that client is someone who never smiled before, it's a wonderful moment. Only a therapist can get so excited.

When she began the program in music therapy at California State, Long Beach, Denise developed proficiency in piano and guitar. "I have yet to see a therapist who does not use a guitar," she says. "It doesn't have to be at a proficient level, but music therapists must be able to read music and play the guitar and piano."

PERFORMING

"As a music therapist, you're not a performer," Denise says, "but many therapists do some level of performing as well as their work in therapy. You *can* do both." She expects to perform, too. "I plan to work in musical theater—community theater, dinner theater."

Denise has a sound suggestion for high school students considering music therapy: Visit a school that offers a music therapy program. Ask to observe, to see what a music therapy session is like. At Cal State, students who are interested in learning more about music therapy can attend a clinic, which includes observation. If you have the opportunity to do that, or to visit a hospital setting to observe therapy, seize the chance. It may help you decide if therapy will be, for you, the best of both worlds.

DANCE THERAPY

For some who love the dance, applause and fame aren't everything. For some, performance means making a difference in someone's life, in changing a life for the better. For some, dance therapy is the right choice.

Dance therapy is a young field: state licensing to practice does not yet exist. Those who perform professionally, however, can become registered by the American Dance Therapy Association. The DTR—Dance Therapist Registered—has met a standard of training and employment that includes either a master's degree from a graduate program in dance therapy or a master's degree in a related field, such as social work, psychology, or counseling. In addition, a clinical internship and several years of paid employment as a dance therapist are required.

Nonverbal Expression

At its essence, dance therapy uses movement to enhance physical and emotional health. The dance therapist may work with a child with a physical disability or an adult with a severe emotional disorder.

The American Dance Therapy Association defines the dance therapist as one who is trained to respond to both the nonverbal and the verbal expressions of a client. The therapist uses knowedge in many areas to achieve this. Among them:

- training in dance, including modern, ballet, folk, and ethnic
- studies in anatomy-psychology, abnormal psychology, kinesiology, and developmental psychology
- experience in dance composition

Mixed Reviews

After winning a master's degree in psychomotor therapy, including an internship at a large state mental hospital, one student was unable to find work in her field. She eventually took a low-paying position as an assistant occupational therapist in a state hospital that did not offer dance therapy to patients. Meanwhile, she attends seminars and plans for the day when she can start her own dance therapy program.

Jobs do exist. Therapists are employed in psychiatric hospitals, clinics, community mental health centers, correctional facilities, and day-care centers. Nursing homes and rehabilitation centers sometimes include dance therapy in their programs.

Because the demand for a dance therapist in most of these situations is low, however, few employ a therapist full-time. Instead, the center may contract with a dance therapist in private practice. The therapist may work at a nursing home one day, a rehabilitation center the next, then on to a day-care facility and back to the nursing home and rehabilitation center. The therapist is self-employed and is concerned with all the business/administrative details involved in self-employment.

Improving the Odds

The American Dance Therapy Association has approved only five programs of study to become a therapist: Antioch/ New England Graduate School (Keene, New Hampshire), Hahnemann Medical College (Philadelphia), Hunter College (New York), New York University, and the University of California in Los Angeles. Other graduate degree programs in dance therapy exist but do not have ADTA approval. Attending a recommended school can improve the dance therapy student's employability.

The professional demands are great. The job outlook is weak. But a dance therapist can make all the difference in the life of a child or adult in need.

CHAPTER 5

ACT ONE: THE THEATER

The dream is the theatre where the dreamer is at once scene, actor, prompter, stage manager, author, audience, and critic.

Carl Jung,
General Aspects of Dream Psychology

As the dream is the theater, the theater is the dream of almost everyone who has tasted the exquisite agony of acting before an audience. A successful performance in a high school play can trigger fantasies of fame on Broadway. Most abandon the dream. Life gets in the way, or the obstacles seem insurmountable. And there are obstacles.

First, there are crowds of other actors with the same dream. About 80 percent of them earn approximately $3,000 a year as actors, according to studies conducted by Actors' Equity and the Screen Actors Guild.

Second, "We need more connoisseurs of culture," as artist Helen Frankenthaler said recently. The demand for live
theater is not strong enough to support the many who seek
roles. Only those who are better than anyone else will get
past the audition.

There are three little words that can make the difference
between becoming a working actor and joining the unemployed: *stay in school.*

THE ACADEMICS OF ACTING

To portray a character on stage, the actor needs an understanding of all of life's conditions. Understanding comes
with knowledge; knowledge comes with learning.

You have begun a career if you are reading every play
you can get your hands on and are analyzing the characters
in the many works of literature you are reading. Reading
and analysis are the first steps in play production: reading
the script, analyzing the characters.

You have begun a career if you are working on college
entrance course requirements. You are paying special attention to English, drama, speech, psychology, social studies, and music.

More than fifteen hundred universities and colleges in
the United States offer undergraduate and/or graduate

degrees in dramatic arts. Studies include the techniques of acting; history of the theater; understanding lighting, scenery, and costumes; analyzing and creating roles; working with directing concepts and techniques; script-study and rehearsal techniques; and lab sessions to gain practical experience. Training in dramatic arts also can be found in specialty schools.

The Academic Edge

Going to the right school can give the actor an edge in a highly competitive field. There are many fine departments of theater at universities and colleges, but some schools have acquired a reputation for producing the best actors. Among them: the Yale Drama School and Carnegie-Mellon University in Pittsburgh.

If you live in a community that supports a high school for the performing arts, you can get an additional academic edge. Wherever you attend high school, however, seek out opportunities to perform in school and in community productions. Plays, talent shows, dramatic readings, and dance production experience help develop skills. Look, too, for opportunities in summer stock, little theater, and children's theater.

Teachers and Mentors

Students of theater arts who are fortunate enough to find a superior teacher, director, or acting coach while in high school have yet another edge. Look for such a mentor—someone who does what you want to do, and does it very well.

Madelyn Berdes, who has enjoyed success with ballet companies as well as in Broadway productions, is still "in school": She is developing her singing voice. With a trio of talents—the ability to dance, sing, and act—her credentials are correct for a theatrical career.

For acting talent alone rarely is enough. Some have enjoyed successful careers without a strong singing voice. And many can neither dance nor even move with grace. But the aspiring actor who can do it all, and do it well, is a triple threat to competitors in a tough business. It's wise to go beyond speech and diction in studying voice. It can pay to go beyond gesture in the study of movement. Learn to sing and dance.

EARNINGS

To create another life through your performance: It's a compelling reason to choose the stage.

You won't do it for the money. About half of the members of the Actors' Equity Association earn nothing by acting in any given year. Of the others, many who earn something do not work long enough to qualify for unemployment. They do other kinds of work to pay the rent, in the theater or elsewhere.

If your heart is set on Broadway, the outlook is especially dour. Opportunities are narrowing on Broadway (which is actually several square blocks in New York rather than a single street). For more than a half century, the classic theater district has steadily diminished. So, too, have the number of available acting roles.

CONTACTS AND CONNECTIONS

To defy the odds of finding work in this shrinking marketplace, you'll need more than talent. You'll need exposure. You'll need friends in high places. In short, it really is not only what you know, but who you know.

This is one reason why attending the right school can boost your prospects. Faculty at noted theater training institutions have professional standing as well as teaching ability. A significant percentage of their students consistently find work in the theater. Some schools have instituted formal programs to introduce graduating actors to directors, casting directors, and agents. *Actor presenta-*

tions, for example, are held annually in New York City during a two-day period. Actors appear in scenes designed to show their talents to the "powers that be" in attendance.

Actor presentations are a feature of member schools of the League of Professional Theatre Training Programs. Among schools that participate are The American Conservatory Theatre, Boston University, The Juilliard School, North Carolina School of the Arts, Temple University, and the University of Washington.

These schools accept students on the basis of audition. Some hold regional auditions at locations throughout the country. To learn more about their requirements, write to the League at 1860 Broadway, Suite 1515, New York, NY 10023.

The drama departments at other schools have fostered careers through connections: Henry Fonda was a member of Princeton's Triangle Club. Cloris Leachman's talent was touted by the faculty at Northwestern University in Evanston, Illinois.

EDUCATION AND TRAINING

Lab Work

Mentors can be found at university theater departments, too. Wouldn't it be nice to be tutored by a famous actor? Or to work with avant-garde artists such as Philip Glass, David Gordon, and members of the Kronos quartet?

Students in the Laboratory for Theatre Research and Performance at UCLA have had this opportunity. The Lab's creator is himself a mentor. Michael Hackett's credentials include directing for the Royal Opera, Covent Garden. Hackett designed the lab for performing arts students in all disciplines, a synthesis of language, voice, music, gesture, and movement. Says Hackett, "The kind of actor I want to develop needs to have a more flexible view of his or her role as a performer. I want to build an artist who can alternate between various styles of acting."

The lab course culminated in a performance workshop. Students spent forty-four hours a week in producing two works of music theater, working with the artists in residence. Professor Hackett underscores the importance of mentors: "It is important for students to work with professional artists.... In music this pattern has existed for years, but in theater it doesn't happen regularly."

Search for a school where it is happening.

The Private School

Look carefully into commercial training—study at an acting school or with a coach. Specialty schools can offer a skill development not found in some college settings. Also, a reputable school can help the talented find roles. Quality in specialty schools varies widely. Investigate before you invest in a program. Schools that have earned fine reputations include The Lee Strasberg Theater Institutes (in Los Angeles and New York City), the Goodman Theatre in Chicago, and the American Academy of Dramatic Arts in New York.

After School

Other than connections made while in school, the Broadway-bound will seek visibility by being there, in the theater district. If you can find theater work (other than acting), you may meet the people who can help you. Dustin Hoffman was once a stage manager.

If paying work isn't available, do volunteer work. Capitalize on the contacts you make. This may disturb the idealist who shelters romantic dreams of being discovered purely on the basis of talent. The reality, however, is this: Broadway theater is business. To be an active part of any business requires knowing the players who make the decisions and letting them get to know you. Theater is no exception.

Away from the Apple

The diminished opportunity on Broadway is the bad news—if it can be called news, given the long history of decline. The good news is diversification and growth in theater throughout the country.

The rules that apply to finding work on Broadway hold true almost everywhere. It's competitive everywhere. But, for the newcomer, the chances of turning an audition into an assignment—and even of getting the audition—improve in smaller markets.

A study conducted by the National Endowment for the Arts identified more than four hundred nonprofit professional theater companies in the United States. Audiences are growing. Many of these regional (or resident) theaters have earned stature and reputation; they do not take second place to Broadway. Further, there is a selective quality in the work performed.

Actors who would be Shakespeareans, who would best like to interpret Beckett, whose joy is Moliere, and who have a passion for the Greek theater can be happiest in regional theater: at the Guthrie in Minneapolis, the American Conservatory in San Francisco, or at one of the younger, energetic companies throughout the country.

THE WORKING ACTOR

First roles may be as a bit player, apprentice, or understudy. From that entry level, it's "just" a cosmic leap to becoming a working actor. Those who make it have accomplished much. They have:

- learned to sing and dance
- acquired poise and good posture
- learned to memorize and mimic
- become adept at movement and gestures that portray character
- practiced and rehearsed past the point of exhaustion
- accepted long hours and low pay
- been flexible in learning, then relearning lines that have been altered after rehearsals
- made a character come alive
- developed stamina, patience, and determination

Latins Anonymous

Successful actors develop a distinctive style. For better or worse, this can lead to typecasting. "I'd delight in being typecast—if only I could be cast," bemoans one struggling would-be in Houston. Other actors struggle with schizophrenia—pretending they are someone they are not—in an effort to avoid being stereotyped.

This was the case for several young actors in Los Angeles. Tired of being called only when the role was for a macho male or a maid named Maria, the actors, of Latin

origin, joined together to write their own script. Rick Na-
jera, Luisa Leschin, Diane Rodriguez, and Armando Mo-
lina wrote *Latins Anonymous*. The show, a comedy made
up of vignettes of Latino experience, premiered at the Los
Angeles Theatre Center after workshop productions at the
Old Globe Theater in San Diego.

With the show's success, the actors now aim to play
leading roles rather than degrading, ethnic supporting
roles; they also have drawn recognition for their writing.
It's a classic case of turning a negative situation into a positive one. It's a testimonial, too, that underscores the attributes needed by actors: imagination, creativity, and
persistence in finding a way, in making an opportunity,
rather than in waiting for it.

Children's Theater

If radio is the theater of the mind, then children's theater
is the theater of the heart. Children's theater is not kids'
stuff: children of all ages—adults included—enjoy imaginative productions staged by companies throughout the
country. Puppets and pantomime are prevalent, but so, too,
are satire, tragedy, classics, and musicals. The Nashville
Academy Theatre, for example, features a wide repertoire—from *The Mikado* to *The Miracle Worker*—and offers a summer theater workshop for students eight to

eighteen. The First All Children's Theatre, in New York, serves as a training center for performers with a talent for musical theater.

Children's theater can be a way to grow, not only for members of the young audience, but for young performers. There are approximately fifty professional companies under the "theater for young audiences" umbrella. Those that run weekly performance schedules may pay performers by the week—usually less than $300. Companies that pay per performance reimburse in the $25 to $40 range. Rarely will an actor find children's theater a sole source of income. For the child-centered performer, however, it can offer great satisfaction.

As of this writing, middle school and high school students in Los Angeles are giving applause to a theater group that weaves racial harmony into Shakespeare.

East L.A. Classic Theatre is doing *Much Ado About Nothing.* With a twist. Musical group Mariachi del Sol has created classic mariachi music and bilingual songs to be woven throughout the play. The cast of twenty-one is made up of adult professionals. Will this be the performers' sole source of income? Not by a long stretch. In fact, it is the actors who make the contribution—in the form of inspiring the community. Says artistic director Tony Plana: "Shakespeare is universal in how he writes about human nature and the human condition. We want kids to go beyond their borders, look at Shakespeare and say, 'That can be mine, too.'

Although it is not financially lucrative, children's theater can bring abundant emotional rewards.

Dinner Theater

"Coughing in the theater is not a respiratory ailment. It is a criticism," said Alan Jay Lerner. What would Lerner say about eating, drinking, smoking, and talking in the theater? More important, how would you handle it?

Dinner theaters, and the audiences they attract, vary enormously. For the actor, it can be a rude awakening to play second place to the *crème brûlée* or the catch of the day. On the other hand, dinner theaters offer opportunities for actors to perform, to gain experience, and to prove professionalism.

They also offer earning potential. Income is based on the theater's size and restaurant capacity. Salaries at *petite* or small theaters (fewer than 400 seats) are in the $300 per performance range; at medium to large houses (400 to 1,000 seats), per-performance pay is nearly $400.

Summer Stock

Another sound training ground for actors is summer stock. Also called the straw-hat circuit, summer theater takes in a broad spectrum of settings from town hall to church basement, from country barn to open-air theater.

Shakespeare himself would have approved of the setting where his work is produced each summer in Ashland, Oregon. Performed under the stars, as the Bard intended, productions at the Oregon Shakespeare Festival provide more theatrical employment, measured in "actor weeks," than any other nonprofit group in the United States. There are about forty Shakespeare summer festivals produced throughout the country, with settings more or less like Ashland's.

Among other summer theaters that offer exceptional performing opportunities are: the Eugene O'Neill Theatre Center, Waterford, Connecticut; the American Shakespeare Festival, Stratford, Connecticut; the Westport Country Playhouse, Westport, Connecticut; the Stratford Shakespeare Festival, Stratford, Ontario.

Acting openings at the crème de la crème are not easily found. Many summer theaters do, however, offer internships for actors.

Salaries in summer stock depend on several factors: whether the company is resident or nonresident stock, theater capacity, and gross profits. Cast members can earn from about $400 to $500 a week, depending on these circumstances. Celebrity "stars," of course, earn more.

If you can find a chance to play "straw-hat," grab it, as you would any opportunity to perform, however lacking in appeal. Breadth of experience cannot be overestimated. The narrow path is the dangerous path—the razor's edge—in almost every career endeavor. This holds especially true for those who want to act.

CHAPTER 6

ACT TWO: TELEVISION AND FILM

Marvelous Truth, confront us
at every turn,
in every guise.

Denise Levertov, *Matins*

So you want to be a star, to be "discovered." Sunglasses and autographs. Big money and fast cars. Have I got a deal for you! Film stars still are discovered. Consider the Casey Siemaszko story.

Director Bill Forsyth was in search of an actor to co-star with Burt Reynolds in *Breaking In*. Forsyth wanted someone young, someone likable, someone who could play the part of an agile, safe-cracking protégé to Reynolds's heavier role.

Eyes glassy after looking at glossy photos of hopeful actors, Forsyth went to an eighteen-screen Hollywood-area movie house, bought a ticket, and began film-hopping: five minutes in one theater, five minutes in another. Finally, after a few minutes of viewing *Biloxi Blues,* it happened: a young soldier, in the background of a barracks shot, waved.

All it took was to be seen. Forsyth scheduled an appointment with Siemaszko at the famous and infamous Château Marmont, where deals are made (and John Belushi died). After reading the script, Siemaszko knew he wanted the role. When the director left to take a phone call, as the story goes, Casey, as edgy as any interviewee, worked off his nervous energy by climbing a tree in the Château's garden. Casey was up a tree when Forsyth returned. "I never figured out if this was just a thing he did, or if he was showing me that he could climb because he knew the character had to do things like that," Forsyth told reporter Daniel Cerone.

All it took was superior "interview skills." Casey Siemaszko was hired. On the surface, the story proves the Hollywood legend: discovery and stardom.

Casey at the Bat

So, at age twenty-eight, Casey Siemaszko is an overnight success. Or is he?

How many small parts had he played before a co-starring opportunity came along? Many. He was a teenage gangster in *Stand By Me.* He played a soldier in *Gardens of Stone* and in *Biloxi Blues.* He was a boxer in *Young Guns* and a 1950s teenager in *Back to the Future.*

Casey Siemaszko also has a college degree in theater arts and made his performance debut at age five, dancing with The Kosciuszko Dancers on Chicago's Polish northwest side. This overnight success is, in fact, a product of a strong, Midwestern work ethic: "Work hard, persevere." While growing up in a culturally active Polish community, Siemaszko acted in local theater and sang in a quartet. He also learned to climb: He would bike to nearby Wrigley Field and scramble up a drainpipe to watch the Cubs.

All it took was a lifetime.

The point, of course, is that being discovered is largely a myth. "The folly of mistaking a paradox for a discovery... is inborn in us," said Paul Valery. For Casey Siemaszko, a film career was years in the making, years made up of experiences and education directed toward a goal.

OPPORTUNITIES AND CREDENTIALS

A surprising number of would-be actors still subscribe to the Hollywood dream without having the credentials: education and experience. Even those who have the credentials are more likely to work at waiting tables than in film. Never mind that some theater arts majors—Ellen Burstyn,

Colleen Dewhurst, Robert Redford, and Paul Newman—
made it. Few do. Jose Ferrar said that "if you want to be an
actor, it has to be the only thing you want to be. If you also
want to be something else, *do* something else."

If you're aware of the reality and rejections ahead, if you
know you have more talent than anyone else, if you're not
bothered by the insecurities, read on to learn where to find
acting jobs.

Bicoastal Conditions

The market for motion picture acting is divided into two
segments: the West Coast is known for feature films, commercials, and television programs; the East Coast specifically New York, for commercials and corporate film and,
of course, soap opera, no small creator of celebrities.

BEING THERE

Whether your destination is New York or Los Angeles,
most of the rules of the road are the same:

1. Take along a college degree in drama and/or a re-
    sume of experiences in summer stock, community
    theater, and the like. It's best to have both.

2. Be prepared for the cost of living. Both New York and Los Angeles are high-rent districts. Survival may depend on finding someone with whom to share an apartment or finding one that is rent-controlled.

3. Join professional organizations. In Los Angeles, the AFI (American Film Institute) offers workshops and seminars. In New York, the National Academy of Television Arts and Sciences (NATAS) can offer opportunities to meet others in the trade. ATAS (Academy of Television Arts and Sciences) in Los Angeles also can be a place for the meeting of like minds. These are nonunion groups.

4. Gather together the essential tools of the trade: the 8-by-10-inch photos and the actor's resume. The photos should not be fantasy shots, but pictures of the real you at your best. The resume is not a business resume, but an actor's dossier of things done. Several books suggest possible formats. (Refer to Appendix A for sources and suggestions.) Your resume will list, in order, your credits, your training, and your special talents. Tape the resume to the back of the photo. If the two are separated, in the eyes of the casting director you exist in only one dimension.

5. Read the trade papers, such as *Back Stage* and *Variety* in New York and *Hollywood Variety* and the *Hollywood Reporter* in Los Angeles. They are of little use in finding a job, but they do describe happenings

in the business. They also are a source of information about producers, directors, casting directors, and future productions.

6. Look into agents. Agents will not find you a job, but they can get you an audition. In New York, having an agent is not always necessary. In Los Angeles, it is. Watch out for help-wanted ads placed by agents: many are phony come-ons. Some are fronts for "acting schools."

7. Keep studying. And become a *quick study*—someone who can sight-read a script effectively. Polish your speaking voice and acting skills in classes or with coaches.

8. Read! Read scripts. Read plays. Read as if you are reading to perform, or you may never have a chance to do so.

BREAKING IN

It's called "The Business" because that's what it is: The film industry is in business to turn a profit. Moviemakers and television producers sell what the public will buy. In much the same way, the actor who aspires to "The Business" needs sales skill. The product is you.

Among the marketing techniques:

1. Begin an organized mailing. Send your photo and resume to reputable agents, casting directors, and any
   contact you make who may be able to help you. Keep
   records of what you sent where and follow up: in person, by phone. In the dictionary, persist is only a page
   away from pest. People will let you know when
   you've crossed the fine line from one to the other, and
   a certain amount of pestiness can play in your favor.
2. Watch for *open calls.* As the term connotes, these are
   auditions open to anyone. *Biloxi Blues,* the film that
   became a calling card for Casey Siemaszko, used an
   open call for casting. A thousand people arrived,
   photos and resumes in hand. On the basis of their
   credentials, some were chosen to audition. And some
   were chosen for roles.
3. Look for commercial breaks. If you can win spots
   playing for commercials, you'll gain experience,
   make yourself visible to people who make film decisions, earn money, and help make yourself eligible to
   join a union.

LOOK FOR THE UNION

Work in commercials can qualify an actor for membership in SAG (Screen Actors Guild). The operant word is

"can." Almost all film actors need this union membership. There are exceptions, as for actors in Texas, a right-to-work state where union membership is not mandatory.

To join SAG, an actor needs to have one of the following qualifications:

1. A commitment to play a principal role for a film, commercial, or filmed television show.
2. Membership, for at least one year, in AFTRA (American Federation of Television and Radio Artists). AFTRA is an open union, meaning that anyone who pays the dues can join, after also paying a weighty initiation fee ($600).
3. Membership, for at least one year, in AEA (Actors' Equity Association). Membership can be obtained through an Equity Membership Candidacy Program in which an actor's work with participating theaters (stock and dinner theaters, for example) builds credit for membership. After fifty weeks of credited work—and payment of a $500 registration fee—an actor is eligible for Equity.

Becoming a member of a union will not help you find work. Unions were formed by and are directed by actors to protect actors in salary negotiations. That is, the unions, having done the negotiating, guarantee that member actors will be paid a minimum salary.

There is a negative side to union membership: Members cannot work with nonprofessionals. If you're still acquiring important experience, union membership will disqualify you from gaining it with community theaters and other places to practice your craft.

WHEN—AND WHAT—IT PAYS

In 1999, the weekly minimum salary for an actor under contract rose to $1,180, according to Actors' Equity studies. Actors in prime-time dramatic television shows of ninety minutes to two hours in length look at incomes near $1,200 per program.

These figures exclude day players (hired for one day only), three-day contracts, special-business performers (action actors without lines), voice-over performers, and extras, all of whom are paid on a separate scale. Celebrity-status actors or their managers negotiate their earnings.

THE VIDEO FACTOR

Suppose that the film in which you had a part goes into videocassette sales. Or it is sold for television use. Actors are entitled to *residuals,* payment for this extended use of a production. Unions have established minimum scales for residual use of a film.

Residuals can be a big deal. Consider that the videocassette recorder is the fastest-selling domestic appliance in history. The huge surge in DVD sales in 1999 can also reflect positively on residuals.

CABLE: CLEARLY DOMINATING

Cable television was developed as a way to give clear reception; today it is the medium of choice for more than half the households in the nation.

The film industry is paying attention. Major producers are creating programs exclusively for cable, among them, Shelley Duvall, Steven Spielberg, and Martin Sheen.

The demand for programming for cable and for superstations produced a new marketplace for the actor. The rules for winning a role are the same as for other film work, already discussed in this chapter. And the competition is no less severe.

Superstations and television networks do offer one different way to get a foot in the door: as a page. Ken Howard did it. A *page* is a temporary worker who usually is given a wide variety of jobs, most of which are menial: delivering scripts, answering phones, and the like. Most important, though, is the chance to learn the business, to see it from a wide spectrum of activities, and to make contacts.

GETTING AN AGENT

As enticing as film and television work may be to the would-be actor, the wise will not be fooled: There is no mystique in the business. There is, however, the need to practice good business: marketing, packaging, promoting, and selling yourself. This also is the work of an agent.

In some film and television markets, the actor must have an agent. Most casting calls and audition calls go out to agents, not directly to actors. There is a catch-22 to this story: The actor almost surely needs the contacts and sales skills of an agent, but it takes contacts and sales skills to get an agent to work for an actor.

Getting work through an agent is not unlike getting work in almost any other area of the economy. You must make a memorable impression. The agent, or agency, that you want to represent you will conduct an interview, review your resume, and discuss your experiences and acting aptitude. But signing an agreement with an agent does not mean you've got the job. It means only that the agent will put in a word for you—if you seem to be right for a role, and if the agent remembers you as the actor who is right for a role. Agents do want to place clients; most receive a 10 percent commission when they do so. But they are most likely to place the client who comes to mind and whose potential earnings will mean 10 percent of a bigger cut.

For this reason, the actor will persistently practice business skills in working with an agent (marketing, packaging, promoting, selling). It goes without saying that the actor will be selling a real talent. The trick is to make that talent apparent. Energy, personality, and appearance are not guarantees of acting ability, but these are criteria often used by agents. Before interviewing with agents, rehearse—preferably with someone who will be a fair and critical judge of how you come across.

After you sign an agreement with an agent, stay in close touch. Continue to seek acting opportunities on your own, too. And know that agents don't get the acting assignments for their clients; they only get them auditions.

The actor who is "better than anyone else," in the eyes of the producer, wins the audition.

NEWS ANCHORS

One of the most brutal armies the world has ever known is on the march again today, just four years after carving a trail of death and destruction through

Central and Eastern Europe.... It's November 18, 1245—and this is *Timeline*.... I'm Stephen Bell.

That's Steve Bell's introduction to a highly unusual version of the evening news. Bell, a former news anchor for ABC's *World News This Morning* and *Good Morning America,* took a similar role for a Maryland Public Television historical reenactment series. Reporting "live" from a contemporary newsroom setting, but sporting medieval costume, Steve Bell called for action reports from field correspondents to cover the last Viking invasion, the Crusades, the Black Death, and other significant events in history. The premise: You are there, watching history in the making, thanks to the miracle of electronics and an innovative public television producer.

Is Bell an anchor or an actor? His capabilities encompass both, but this clearly is a role, and Bell was hired to perform it just as actors were hired to perform other roles in the elaborate *Timeline* productions.

It is not unusual for a media personality to engage in a *layered career*—acting, announcing, sometimes advertising. Bell's primary job is news anchor for KYW–TV in Philadelphia, a position he has held since 1987. He also is national correspondent for Westinghouse Broadcasting. He has been a combat correspondent in Vietnam and, as a thirty-year veteran of broadcast journalism, witnessed the 1968 assassination of presidential candidate Robert Kennedy.

He served, too, as a White House correspondent during the final months of Watergate.

Bell's career path is not typical, but it is representative of the kinds of experiences that lure people to this highly visible arena.

Salary

The anchor, or TV newscaster, reports news, introduces other on-air reports, and is the focal point of a newscast. In many communities, the TV anchor achieves celebrity status. Top personalities receive more than $1 million a year from the major networks that employ them. An anchor, like an actor, is considered a talent. As such, the popular anchor is a commodity, one who may be sought and bought to bring bigger consumer audiences to a station.

Which brings us to the less glamorous aspects of this sought-after career:

1. First, ratings wars create a battleground for anchors. According to the Radio-Television News Directors Association (RTNDA), the annual job turnover rate is as high as 25 percent.
2. Although a high turnover for announcing positions would seem to indicate more opportunities, the com-

petition is so intense that opportunities are scarce. A small percent of reporters become anchors

3. While the million-dollar anchors draw headlines, the average annual salary for an anchor in a top market is about one-tenth that—$100,000. Anchors at small stations may be paid $25,000 a year, or less.

Skin Deep? Or Tough Skinned?

As for acting, success for an anchor can depend heavily on an attractive appearance and engaging delivery. Other credentials include a college degree with extensive courses in English, speech, and political science. Many anchors have been speech, journalism, communications, or political science majors. Graduate degrees are preferred. The anchor should have an ability to identify events, analyze their impact, and report on them in a way that will be understandable to a wide viewing audience. Almost all anchors begin in small markets, and almost all worked as reporters and newswriters before they were named for a top broadcast job.

For all the glamor attributed to their position, anchors also are subject to criticism, called "talking heads," and accused of airing "dirty laundry."

There is also the possibility of becoming yesterday's news. Christine Craft, a Kansas City anchor, sued her employers. The reason? She was fired, she claimed, because she no longer was attractive enough for the job.

For some, TV news anchor is a short-term career. Christine Craft challenged the decision, then went on to other things. She became the news director of a Sacramento, California, television station. With far more attributes than an attractive physical appearance, she pushed her career into long-term status.

Would-be anchors with integrity and skill, who not only look good, but *are* good, have the attributes for real success in the long run.

CHAPTER 7

DANCE: CLASSICAL, MODERN, AND MORE

Dancing is the loftiest, the most moving, the most beautiful of the arts because it is no mere translation or abstraction from life; it is life itself.

Havelock Ellis,
The Dance of Life

All the world's a stage for today's professional dancer. Although the Big Apple still is a bastion of classical dance in America, the cultural iron curtain has cracked, too. Rather than diminishing New York, this change enhances the entire sphere of dance. From New York City to San Francisco, and at hundreds of points in between, dance lives.

DANCE COMPANIES

Performers of both ballet and modern dance can work as part of dance and opera companies. These staged productions can draw the best dancers and demand an exacting discipline from them. The directors/choreographers of these companies, like the legendary Balanchine (New York City Ballet) or San Francisco's young whiz, Helgi Tomasson, run a kind of benevolent dictatorship.

Some dancers are drawn to this demanding perfection. Patricia McBride, principal dancer at the New York City Ballet for twenty-eight years, cherishes the memory of working for a vigorous and rigorous director: "It was like the whole company was dancing for him."

Toni Bentley, in her insightful book *Winter Season: A Dancer's Journal,* describes the power George Balanchine exerted over the dancers:

> Most women have two important men in their lives—their father and their lover. We have three. Mr. Balanchine is our leader, our president, our mother, our father, our friend, our guide, our mentor, our destiny. He knows all, sees all, and controls all....

While there are degrees of such dictatorship—and of benevolence—in dance companies, expect to find rigorous uniformity in classical dance. This does not mean the dancer loses individuality, necessarily. Helgi Tomasson is noted for choosing dancers with distinctive styles. Patricia McBride reports that if Balanchine liked you, he trusted you to be yourself and did not try to change you into something you were not.

Still, one rule is inflexible: The choreographer/director is in command.

MUSICAL THEATER

Musical theater offers another venue for the classically trained dancer, one which also is not limited to the Broadway stage. Madelyn Berdes, a member of the ballet chorus for the long-running theatrical production of *Phantom of the Opera* (soon to play in a movie theater near you), explained why she left company dance for the theater:

> I got tired of ballet companies and the restrictions which come with them. Shows seem to be the next step. They pay just as well, the type of people involved are not solely ballet dancers, but actors and singers. It's a great opportunity to extend one's abilities.

Lively, lovely, and headstrong, the Milwaukee-born Berdes has performed with New York's Joffrey Ballet and Feld Ballet, as well as four years in Cologne, West Germany, and Zurich, Switzerland. When did she first set her career sights on the dance?

> I started taking ballet classes at about eight years old, but didn't get serious about it until I was sixteen or seventeen. An older professional dancer gave me encouragement, and that meant a lot.

Madelyn Berdes's words mirror a truism for dancers: Almost all begin dance classes by age eight. Preballet training can start earlier. Most have more than one lesson a week, practice daily, and have made a career decision to dance by the time they are sixteen or seventeen—often much earlier. (Most professional companies audition dancers for professional jobs when the dancers are seventeen or eighteen.) Further, dancers remain students throughout their careers. Even the most gifted and experienced take class daily.

THE DILEMMA OF A SHORT-TERM CAREER

Madelyn Berdes's decision to dance in musical theater has broad implications. She wants to develop her singing voice. She has her antennae up, watchful for new opportunities—in the theater or out of it. She knows that dance can be a short-term career. It calls for extraordinary energy, agility, and strength. These qualities are not exclusive to the young, but most dancers cannot maintain them.

Some choose teaching. Others become choreographers. A few find other professional performing opportunities in the theater, as actors or singers. For those with strong social sensibilities, a career in dance therapy can be rewarding. (See Chapter 4 for music-related therapeutic work.)

CAREER OPTIONS FOR DANCERS

Emerging options in dance are available to the retired performer as well as to others with dance ability, a working knowledge of music and movement in dance, and an exceptional attention to detail.

Dance companies hire *movement notators*. Notators record a dance using graphic symbols, called labanotation. They produce a graphic score. The score includes graphic notation of the movement, music, costume sketches, background notes, and as many other details as are required to restage a performance. Notators need basic technical dance training, but need not be performers. They do need a broad general education and notation courses from a college or university or from the Dance Notation Bureau. Notator training from the bureau includes an apprenticeship, as well as courses in notator speed-writing and work on an independent project.

Movement notators also work in dance libraries and for college and university dance departments.

Reconstructors work with dance notation. A reconstructor trains a dance company to perform a dance notated in score form. Most have been professional performers, and all have the ability to direct people. Reconstructors have had extensive training in the system of notation. Typically, a reconstructor will have taken a ballet master's workshop with the Dance Notation Bureau.

Autographers put notation into a readable typographical format that can be published. Today, computer-prepared scores help make labanotation available to more dancers. Autographers are trained in dance notation.

Growth in dance notation makes it possible for a choreographer to receive payment when someone buys a published, notated copy of his or her performance or when someone performs the dance. Dance notation ensures that a performance can be not only memorable, but recorded, down to the finest detail, so it can be danced again and again.

THOROUGHLY MODERN DANCER

Modern dance, an American-born art form, owes much to Isadora Duncan. She breathed new spirit into dance when she broke with the classical traditions of ballet. That spirit is still very much alive.

The modern dancer has technical skills in ballet, but the technique of modern dance is comparatively free and creative. Both styles of dance use some of the same techniques. Both require disciplined study. But modern dance is marked by experimentation, by the avant-garde, by multimedia productions that go beyond dance.

Words such as "witty," "playful," even "comical" often are used to describe modern dance performances. The employment picture for dancers, however, is anything but funny. As in ballet, work is irregular and seasonal. Even the most established dancers rarely look forward to more than thirty-six weeks of performing during a year. Further, modern dance is marked by a constantly shifting scene: New companies are born, old ones dissolve. Companies depend on sponsors even more heavily than do ballet companies.

On the plus side, the performing life of the modern dancer usually is somewhat longer than is that of the ballet dancer. Nevertheless, the odds for achievement in this tiny, capricious field are disappointing.

Wizard of Odds

What are the odds for a corn-fed seventeen-year-old from Kansas City, Missouri, to make it in modern dance? David Parsons is a wizard of odds.

Parsons took a soaring occupational leap when he was selected as a member of the celebrated Paul Taylor Dance Company. For nine years, Parsons was the company's principal dancer. Just when others would say he'd reached relative stardom, Parsons quit to begin his own company. Then he broke a bone in the bottom of his foot.

Was it over? David Parsons couldn't dance, but he could choreograph. He had, in fact, choreographed his first dance at age seventeen. The David Parsons Dance Company went on, without Parsons in performance. Says Parsons: "People don't just want me; they want my dances."

That is success for a man who always believed that dancing and choreography go hand in hand. For Parsons, the transition from the demands of the dance to the demands of artistic direction is just right.

CHOREOGRAPHING A CAREER

To become a choreographer or dance director, it is not essential to have been a performer, although many have danced professionally. It *is* important to have technical knowledge and performance background in many dance forms, as well as expertise in music, costuming, lighting, and staging. This is an administrative position, as well. It calls for management skills: the ability to motivate people, the ability to promote the product, and, in some cases, the ability to handle financial and administrative paperwork.

Creative imagination and choreography are practically synonyms. Yet, without a sound educational background, the future choreographer is handicapped. To be able to communicate "life itself," requires a knowledge of life. For this reason, a broad liberal arts education, as well as studio or college courses in choreography, are recommended. The choreographer is well acquainted with literature, languages, visual arts, and music as well as dance. Armed with all of these, along with the stamina, enthusiasm, self-discipline, and perseverance that is part of all performing arts, choreographers can find a place with companies, in television and video, with the theater, and in film.

ETHNIC PERFORMANCE

It is said that a Native American, on meeting a member of another tribe, would not say, "Who are you?" but rather, "What do you dance?"

Dance is a part of every culture. The perfomance of a dance is a central feature of some of Native Americans' most profound religious ideas: the Sun Dance of renewal, the Ghost Dance.

Dance that is associated with a particular people and cultural heritage offers a unique translation of life. Companies specialize in European folk dance, Spanish dance, Irish (river) dance, African, Afro-American, Native American, or any of many other national styles. Dancers for these companies may be professionals, in the sense that they are paid to perform. Most, however, are paid very little. They dance because they love the dance. Earnings usually go to defray costs of travel and costumes. Ethnic dancing can be a spirited avocation, but seldom a vocation.

JAZZ DANCE

Jazz dancing calls for some of the training found in ballet and modern dance, as well as acting and singing ability. Most dancers who work in musicals, night clubs, dinner theaters, movies, and television have been trained in jazz dance. Although there are a few organized jazz companies, most jazz dancers work as freelancers: They audition for every new show or opportunity.

The settings and work conditions for jazz dance are very different from those for ballet, modern, and most ethnic dance performances. The atmosphere of a smoky nightclub featuring jazz dance routines in a review is unlike that of a theater, where the audience has come to focus on the performance. In a nightclub, the dance is a diversion accompanied by conversation and drinks. If smoke and laughter hinder your serious performance, jazz dancing may not interest you.

TINY DANCER: DANCE STATISTICS

Dance attracts more women than men. Professional dancers hold an average of about ten thousand positions at any given moment. That's a tiny figure, even when compared to other competitive performing careers.

Of those ten thousand dancers, about 90 percent are women. Because many dance companies hire an equal number of men and women, the competition for women is nine times as intense as it is for men. And it's very competitive for men.

Dancers who belong to the American Guild of Musical Artists earn salaries that range from $543 a week for new performers to $693 for principal dancers. The ballet chorus (or corps dancers) earn an average of $600 a week.

Income for choreographers and artistic directors varies wildly, from as little as $1,000 a week to six figures per year.

NATIONAL PERFORMANCE NETWORK

Do you want to dance? The National Endowment for the Arts (an independent agency of the federal government) sponsors a National Performance Network. Its purpose is to help link independent performing artists and small companies with performing opportunities throughout the country. Within its dance program, a special grant has been awarded to the Dance Theatre Workshop. For more information, contact the Dance Theatre Workshop, 219 West 19th Street, New York, NY 10011.

DANCING TO A DIFFERENT DRUMMER

Phantom dancer Madelyn Berdes, whose dance career spans a variety of settings, says that the performance highlight of her life was dancing in Juri Kylian's *Transfigured Night* with the Joffrey. "It's one of the most demanding ballets, yet very satisfying and beautiful." While she cherishes the memory, she recognizes the universe of dance: Joy can be found in a wide range of performance arenas. Asked to give her personal words of wisdom for young dancers, she responds:

> Start early and get a strong basis in dance, singing, or acting. Get as much basic training as possible and ex-

perience with on-stage performing. Don't limit yourself to 'thinking technical.' Every experience you put
yourself through is one to learn from. Watch the
other performers. Use your eyes and absorb what
their years of experience have taught them.

Don't be afraid of trying something new, perhaps
making a fool of yourself or falling on your face.
Don't be afraid! Have confidence in yourself and do
your individual best in whatever career you choose.
Maintain your individuality.

In *Dance and the Soul,* Paul Valery wrote, "All of her
was love! And that is why only a dancer can make it visible
by the beauty of her actions."

CHAPTER 8

THE UPBEAT AND THE OFFBEAT: OTHER WAYS TO PERFORM

Have you heard the one about…the guy who tells stories for a living? It's a performance art of another hue.
Len Cabral is one of The Spellbinders, a group of story-
tellers who perform in schools, for youth programs, and
at arts festivals. With an extraordinary imagination and a
gift for mime, he most enjoys inventing and performing
"healing stories," the kind that make kids feel better
about themselves.

The number of offbeat ways to work as a performer is
limited only by imagination. Over the years, *Career World*
magazine has featured a wide variety of unusual performers in the monthly "Offbeat Job" column. Their stories are
significant, not because some are weird or funny or spec-
tacular or attention-getting, but because all show an inven-
tiveness on the part of the performer. The stories say, too,

that you need not be locked into traditional ways to work; given their creative, yet disciplined natures, students of performing arts can be especially in tune with the possibilities, many of which are entrepreneurial.

As unreal as some may seem, the following tales are true. They are offered as a catalyst: to trigger your imagination in thinking about enterprising ways to sell your talent.

PERFORMERS

THE SERGEANT

Paul Cole marches to the beat of his own drum—and to the twenty-eight other instruments he totes. As "Sergeant Pepperoni," Cole is a one-man band. He plays at fairs, during football halftimes, and in schools. Cole was once a serious student of music who sang and composed opera, and he worked with Leonard Bernstein. Cole says, "Some people try to find a career: I like to think it is also possible to create a career for yourself." He also creates instruments. His "Sousaflush" is a bugle made from a toilet bowl and two feet of copper tubing. Even when hauling one hundred pounds of instrumental metal on a hot, summer Sunday, Sergeant Pepperoni has as much fun as his audience.

THE CAPTAIN

If you can get past Richard Pesta's stage name, you'd really like him. As Captain Sticky, caped crusader, he wants the world to be a better place. Wearing a gold cape and boots and a shiny "S" on his T-shirt, he draws attention to himself and to the social problems he campaigns against. He searches out bad conditions in nursing and rest homes. He attacks unfair or misleading advertising. If he doesn't like what he finds, he just might zap the wrongdoers with a blast of peanut butter from his "stickygun." He keeps himself in peanut butter by making and selling his own brand of the stuff—natural peanut butter, of course.

OTHER CRUSADERS

Good nutrition is the mission of Vita-Woman and Nutri-Man. As Mary Lopez and John Doyle, the actors went to work for the New York State Department of Health. The dynamic duo visit elementary and junior high school classrooms, where they show kids how to eat well and tell them to avoid junk food. In costume, these heralds of health present fitting, and physically fit, role models.

RINGMASTER

Jonathon Lee Iverson, just twenty-four, is the youngest ringmaster ever for the "Greatest Show on Earth," Ringling Bros. and Barnum & Bailey Circus. A former member of the Boys Choir of Harlem, Iverson brings a powerful tenor voice to his new role in the center ring. The classically trained New Yorker says: "Artistry is artistry. Art is about communicating, period.... My main thing is doing what I do well," he told freelancer Libby Slate.

COUNTERTENOR

Bejun Mehta gave up a distinguished career as a boy soprano at age fifteen, when his voice changed. Wanting to remain in music, he tried to sing baritone, with little success. In 1997, the twenty-nine-year-old found his voice: singing in falsetto. As a male soprano, Mehta has been booked for the Chicago Lyric, Santa Fe Opera, San Francisco Opera, and the New York City Opera. His schedule, through 2001, includes the role of Tolomeo in Handel's *Giulio Cesare* at the L.A. Opera. Amazed by his own success, Mehta says: "Oh my God, I'm an opera singer."

COACH

She works out with the Cleveland Browns. Roni Mahler, a *regisseur* (theatrical director) of the Cleveland Ballet, brought the dance to the football team's workout routine. She decided to train players in dance exercises to improve their balance and make them less injury-prone. An off-season coach, many of Mahler's stretches and leaps became a regular part of the players' warm-up routines.

CHIMNEY SWEEP

David Stoll and Dee Miller work in costume and are adept at dance. Their stage, however, is a rooftop. Their work: chimney sweeping. With a taste for the dramatic, Stoll started a sweep school, featuring both classroom study and on-roof training.

COMPUTERIZED MUSIC

Robb Murray has a way to blend interests in music and computers—using creativity as a cement. He makes music on a microcomputer. Besides composing and programming, he does his own recording, advertising, and promotion. He goes for baroque—playing a recorder, mandolin, organ, and fifteenth-century harpsichord—a form, he says, that reproduces well electronically.

STUNTWOMAN

The traditional pre-performance line to wish an actor well—"break a leg"—would not sit well with Jadie David. David is a stuntwoman. An athlete, dancer, and expert rider, David was "discovered" while riding her horse near her parents' home on Los Angeles parkland. She was asked to be a double—a stand-in in the saddle for a film star. Although horse riding stunts were her favorite, after riding bareback for two weeks for *Charlie Chan and the Dragon Lady,* David welcomed other performing opportunities.

STREET MUSICIAN

Bob Devlin was an out-of-work musician when he decided playing for handouts was better than not playing at all. He'd pick places and times to perform where people were most likely to pass by and contribute to his livelihood: lunch hour on payday, for example. His skills as a street musician opened up avenues to perform inside jobs. He has played at congressional parties, at schools, even at the White House.

SHOW-TO-GO

Paul Mackley performs one-man shows in living rooms, cafés, parks, and prisons. His ninety-minute production, Wallace Shawn's *The Fever,* was recently performed in a car, while the audience of one drove around Los Angeles. "It was difficult without a dressing room," said Mackley. He gets as many as five gigs a week, most of them house calls at parties.

VOICE-OVERS

He's the voice for Mr. Peanut, Reddy Kilowatt, and dozens of other characters. Karl Kraft, an actor, narrator, on-camera announcer, and impressionist, is also a talking cartoon. He gave up Broadway to work at trade shows, fairs, and amusement parks. Hidden behind a booth, he is the voice for an animated cartoon character on video. He holds conversations—most of which are punctuated with stand-up comic humor—with passersby. He makes teaching cassettes and does voice-overs for advertising characters.

From Murder to Magic

ACTORS

Experiential theater—of the sort that murder-mystery weekends are made—has become a popular, if unusual business for entrepreneurs with a taste for the dramatic. David Greenberg and David Landau are two such professional premeditators. They run Murder to Go, Inc. Their interactive murder mystery parties are staged at hotels and for cruise lines. They write the stories, set the stage, and direct professional actors, who bring the productions to life (or death!).

CLOWNS

Be a clown? Dean Steed did. He's a horseback-riding clown of a different color: He works rodeos. His costumes, acrobatics, and bad jokes all fall into the circus-clown category. A large part of his work, however, is dead serious: When a cowpoke falls and is in danger of being gored by a bull, it's Steed's job to get in the ring and distract the bull, getting it to run after Steed instead. How does he do that?

By slapping the bull in the face! Performing careers can carry some unusual risks.

MAGICIANS

Ehrich Weiss made his professional debut in Appleton, Wisconsin, then changed his name. As Harry Houdini, he was the inspiration for many careers in magic. One of his followers, Chuck Stanford, has carved out an unusual niche as a magician. He works trade shows. Earning an average of $1,000 a day, he draws in customers for the companies who hire him. His stage: a convention booth.

Who's Who: From Animal to Zoo

What does an unemployed actor do between jobs? One became a real animal. And he was paid for it. Albert Vidal, actor and mime, went on exhibit at a zoo. He shared a pen with a Galapagos tortoise. Both Vidal and the turtle were tended by zookeepers. Vidal said he wanted to present "the city dweller in a harmonious setting with some of the world's other creatures." The description on Vidal's cage read: "Found in cities throughout the planet, Homo sapiens urbanus; territory extends to places like high rises, discos, and fast-food restaurants."

The territory for performance artistry extends far beyond traditional boundaries. Following is a sample of other creative performance-related careers:

- Professional mimic Rick Huff does vocal impressions, mostly for radio advertising. For one commercial he was the entire cast of *The Wizard of Oz*.
- An actress and playwright, Leigh Curran became involved with a nonprofit outreach program targeting at-risk youth in New York. After several volunteer years, she started a similar program in Santa Monica, California, called the Virginia Avenue Project. Original productions are performed by kids, each of whom has a volunteer mentor. The project does thirty plays a year with the help of fifty "at-risk" children and their mentors, who have included Amy Brenneman (*Your Friends & Neighbors*) and Winnie Holzman (creator of *My So-Called Life*).
- The man who created the sound of laser guns for *Star Wars* is Ben Burtt, sound effects designer for Lucasfilm. He knows the importance of sound in drama and chooses "the sound with the right texture or emotion."
- Madge Hurrah, pianist and composer, makes made-to-order accompaniments for women gymnasts. They literally flip for her music.
- A "theater gypsy" who made costumes for her nine brothers and sisters before earning a degree in theater

arts, Mary Stromberg is now a professional costume maker. Her business draws big-business clients, who use Stromberg's animal costumes in advertising and promotion.

• Carie De Ruiter designs titles for movies. To find the right look for the letters, she may consult with the composer to match the title to the music or with the film editor to match title to opening footage.

• When she isn't making TV commercials or playing bit parts, you can see Gwen Adair in the ring. She's a boxing referee.

• And then there's Mike MacDonald, entreprenerd. MacDonald's Rent-a-Nerd business is booming. He rents himself out. Dressed as a nerd and acting the part with math-grad accuracy, MacDonald plays Hornby K. Fletcher at parties. He's performing. He's having fun. He's earning a living.

BUT IS IT ART?

When Garrison Keillor talks, people listen. Keillor brought *A Prairie Home Companion* from radio to stage. His "annual farewell" performance, from the stage of the Universal Amphitheatre in Universal City, is broadcast live, coast-to-coast, via public radio.

Keillor's kind of folk-art storytelling, with its appeal to a wide audience, has a parallel in performance poetry. A growing form, it evolved from poetry-reading sessions to poetry reading accompanied by music and dance. Today it can include "theatrical adventures," as Julian Neil calls the perfomances he directs. Actors take over for the poets. In one production, Neil edited the work of eight poets, then combined their works into a single story line. Neil's intent was to bring poetry to a wider audience, including those who may not normally read it.

Is it art? Some theater critics—whose job, after all, is to be critical—may say that productions such as Keillor's or Neil's do not meet the standards of the legitimate theater. But this is a new century. Fewer people listen to the old standards. And you have your own standards for performance. Offbeat or otherwise, that's what counts.

CHAPTER 9

THE DEVELOPING CAREER: AUDITIONS, INTERVIEWS, BIOS

My fingers sweat, my lips quiver, I can't breathe, I get saliva in my mouth. It's like everything collapses on itself and I become a little mass of quivering flesh trying to get through, trying to concentrate… There's no rhyme or reason. I just have to practice not thinking about it.

Stan Savant,
All in a Day's Work

You can't always get what you want. Most positions in performing arts call for an audition; some also call for an interview. You can't always be among the chosen, no matter how much you want the job. The competition is too severe, in all areas of the arts.

But if you try, sometimes, you'll get what you need: an opportunity to perform, to be seen, to be heard. If you approach each audition as just that, nothing more, you're less likely to tie yourself up in knots, to experience some of the performance symptoms so aptly described by Stan Savant, flutist, in an interview with photojournalist Neil Johnson. (Johnson's insightful book, *All in a Day's Work: Twelve Americans Talk About Their Jobs,* was published by Little, Brown & Company, Boston, in 1989, but it is still relevant today.)

AUDITIONS ARE AWFUL

Here is what Stan Savant had to say about the audition process:

> Today most orchestras—major, minor, and Podunk— announce positions in a paper called *International Musician.* You send in a resume, maybe a tape, and if you're asked to audition, you go, at your own expense, and sit behind a screen with a small committee of orchestra personnel out front listening. The playing is totally anonymous. It's terrifying! One little foul-up and you're out. There are so many fine artists who cannot find jobs. Hundreds of people in the United States could do my job. But they can't find work. Many are waiting tables in New York or Los Angeles.

One modest sentence in Savant's statement is all-important for the young performer to remember: *Hundreds of people in the United States could do my job.* If you're serious about performing, you could audition many, many times as your career develops. If you don't win the job at an audition, it may not have anything to do with your ability as a performer. You could, perhaps, do the job as well as, or better than, the one who won.

This is because auditions, like life itself, are not always fair. This is not to say that auditions are intentionally *unfair;* rather, they are simply a reflection of human judgment and are further bound by the dictates of available dollars. The people who make performance decisions have all kinds of things to consider: funding, budgets, and travel costs among them. They may have liked your performance, but were unable to hire you. And, as the Central Opera Service suggests in guiding young performers, very often there are differences of opinion among those who are judging you. A director may acquiesce to the preference of a conductor; a conductor may give way to the choice of a general manager; a casting director may step back when a producer voices a choice; a director may reach a compromise with a producer.

The final decision may leave you out of the running, but it does not mean that there were not positive reactions to your performance. You can't please everybody all the time.

Is It Better to Be First—or Last?

Other factors influence decision making at auditions. Among them: Is it better to be the first performer or the last?

The candidate who is first, and who does very well, becomes a kind of benchmark performer. Everyone who follows is measured against Number One. On the other hand, the strong, fresh performer who makes the closing appearance may succeed in erasing the memory of all who have gone before.

Being Rejected

To compound audition woes, another performer may have worked for the producer/director/manager in a previous production and thus may have gained a critical edge. Or, another performer may know the producer/director/manager. The off-stage alliance can hurt your chances, but it has nothing to do with your ability. Don't let it discourage you. Instead, work to enhance your chances.

Become known. Word of mouth can be very important. Every audition you attend is an opportunity. Producers and managers who like you may let others know about you. It also is possible that you'll be rejected for a role at hand as an actor, dancer, or singer, but that the producers will be considering you for another role in a future production, one for which they think you are better suited.

Being Cast

The advice given to young singers from the Central Opera Service can serve in many performance areas: Most important, be professional. Find out as much as you can about who you will be performing for, what the producers' plans are, and what performances they are trying to cast.

If you are a singer, a musician, or a dancer, choose something you know you do well, but be ready to do a variety of selections in a variety of styles.

If you are an actor, you will have read and rehearsed a variety of sample scripts, monologues, and dialogues, until you have become familiar with a wide range of materials in the medium in which you intend to succeed. In short, you'll be ready for anything when the script is handed to you. Being prepared is the best way to fight off the nervous symptoms Stan Savant described.

About nerves: Everyone experiences them. Expect to be nervous, and use your nervousness to advantage, if you can. In most cases, a nervous audition is better than a bland one. If you are able to direct nervous energy into performing energy, "nerves" can be a great advantage, rather than a handicap.

HIGH-PERFORMANCE RESUMES

When you arrive for an audition, have your photographs, resumes, or other biographical information with you. The material will have been prepared as professionally as you can make it. The format for biographical information differs from one area of the performing arts to another—and also differs within an area. For example, the resume for an actor looking for a role in theater in New York will differ from that of an actor looking for film work in Los Angeles.

Both resumes will be neatly and accurately typed and artfully arranged on a single page. Both typically will be attached to a professional 8-by-10-inch photograph. Both will put your name and your union affiliations first, followed by your phone number and the name and phone number of your agent. And both resumes will list vital statistics (weight, height, hair color, eye color) just below the union affiliations.

At this point, the resumes diverge: Both go immediately into credits, but the Broadway-bound actor lists theater credits first, beginning with the strongest. For example:

THEATER:

Broadway:	*Title of Play*	Role Played	Other Roles/ Understudy
Off-Broadway:	*Title of Play*	Role Played	Where Played
	Title of Play	Role Played	Where Played
Stock:	*Title of Play*	Role Played	Where Played

Theater credits are followed by film credits:

FILM:	*Title of Film*	Role Played	Name of Producer/ Film Company

Film credits are followed by television credits, then commercial work, if any, and print advertising where it is appropriate.

For the actor in Los Angeles, film, television, and commercial credits are listed before theater credits.

The format for both resumes then follows a similar form. Both list training (where you went to school and for how long, degrees earned, significant mentors/directors) followed by a list of special skills and abilities that apply, or could apply, to acting. Some examples include the ability to dance, listing forms (ballet and/or modern, for example); the ability to sing, including a credit for voice study; the ability to ice-skate, roller skate, hang glide, ride a horse, do freestyle Frisbee, or anything else that you do well and that could—realistically—help you win an audition.

There are a number of very good sources on resume writing, such as *Resumes for Performing Arts Careers,* published by VGM Career Books. Be sure to follow a format specifically designed for your field. Unlike the resumes for business, information will never be listed chronologically, will not state your objectives or career goals, and will not specify salary expectations. And ask others to critique your resume, especially if they have had experience in evaluating resumes of performing artists—and in making a decision for a role.

Mail Call

Beyond having your resume with you when you go to an audition or interview, you will be sending it to a wide range of people who could help you in a job search. Depending on your field, these can include agents, producers, directors, casting directors, managers, conductors, choreographers, and anyone who could put in a good word for you.

These may include teachers, school alumni, friends who know people in the performing arts, friends who are active in the performing arts, and arts acquaintances who need to be reminded of who you are.

Always include a cover letter with your resume (and photograph, where applicable). This brief letter will introduce you, tell why you are sending this resume, and, if it is appropriate to do so, will ask for an appointment or interview.

If you have an audiotape or videocassette of your performing talent, say so in your cover letter. Unless you have been specifically asked to include a tape, do not send it with your resume. Unsolicited videos and performance tapes can be a costly venture—and they may not be played.

Role Call

Keep a record of everyone to whom you send a resume. Follow through with a postcard or brief letter to ask whether your resume has been received and to remind the recipient of who you are. Even if the responses you get are not favorable, keep this record of contacts. There may come a time when it is correct to try again, perhaps with a different approach, or when you have added experience to your credentials.

If your performance portfolio—resume, photograph, and, possibly, a follow-up audiotape or video—wins you an interview or audition, rejoice. Do your professional best; then forget about the role, and go on to your next project.

It does little good to sit next to a phone waiting for a role call, to dwell on what you think you should have done. Performing artists need resiliency, a real talent for recovery and resurrection. Take what you learned from the last audition and move toward the next. Each opportunity to be seen and heard adds to your storehouse of knowledge and widens the circle of those who know of you.

Auditions are awful. But they lead to roles. And, almost always, you will be performing for people who love music or theater or film or the dance as much as you do. They are your audience. Entertain them.

CHAPTER 10

THE FUTURE IN PERFORMING ARTS: NET EFFECT

The bottom line of technology is, "What are you communicating?" And that's still more important to me than *how* you're communicating.

Bono, U2

A brave new world is here. Until the next massive technological change appears, we can count on the Internet as a factor and a force in our lives.

Most think this is a good thing.

Michael Stipe, of R.E.M., puts it this way: "It could really destroy the system that's set up now. I think that's really healthy."

MUSIC: FROM PIRATES TO PUBLICITY

Some think we are crossing forbidden boundaries with the Web. Pirates, many college students using sophisticated on-campus programs, are using high-speed Internet access to swap and trade illegally copied music. Geoff Boucher, writing for the *Calendar,* poses provocative questions in light of these developments: Does this mark the twilight of the major record labels? Can piracy be stopped? Should artists see the Internet as a wide, liberating landscape, or just a new way to get lost in the crowd?

For would-be artists seeking a way to break in, the Internet is Oz: full of promise. Singer-songwriter Randy Newman believes it doesn't hurt to give away a song: "Anything to get people to notice me is of use to me," he told Boucher.

In tomorrow's world, artists who today record an album and hope for record sales would instead, perhaps, record a song a month. The Internet would hold a vast library of music from artists able to launch their careers at very little cost. They would by-pass the record labels entirely, going straight to one of the new music websites that open almost daily.

FILM: THE DVD PIRATE WARS

Piracy is a factor in film, too. In January 2000, the film industry won a major battle in its war against online piracy.

A federal judge ordered websites to stop distributing De-CSS, a program that can be used to make pirate copies of DVD movies.

Jack Valenti, chief executive of the Motion Picture Association of America, called the ruling "a great victory for creative artists, consumers, and copyright owners."

Online activists, however, sing a different tune. "This will have a chilling effect on free speech," said Robin Gross, speaking for the Electronic Frontier Foundation. Others in the Internet community believe the federal ruling is a lost cause because the De-CSS program has already spread out of control.

One thing is certain: This is only the beginning of the Web battles. And while the future is not certain, it seems to bode better for performers than the status quo.

GROWTH AREAS AND CHANGING OPPORTUNITIES

As promising as the "Net effects" may be, they do not represent the entire drama of developments in the performing arts.

The Actors' Equity Association announced, just before the century turned, an all-time high in membership and in member earnings. (See chart.)

The association, the official representative of theatrical performers for eighty-seven years, has been a champion for

Thirty-Year Overview

	1998–99	1997–98	*1993–94	1988–89	1978–79	1968–69
Weekly Employment, # of members	5,802	5,547	4,712	4,442	3,950	3,060
Principal, per week	3,650	3,575	3,013	3,010	2,730	2,081
Chorus, per week	1,372	1,270	1,151	709	599	604
Stage Manager, per week	751	688	602	631	517	358
% Employed, per week	15.3%	15.4%	14.3%	12.2%	15.4%	21.1%
Earnings						
Median Annual Earnings	$6,261	$6,276	$5,371	$4,636	$2,562	N/A
Average Annual Earnings	$14,936	$14,936	$12,568	$9,676	$6,365	$3,699
Total Annual Earnings (millions)	$244.0	$232.2	$178.0	$137.9	$75.9	$36.9

* = 53-week season

Source: Actors' Equity Association, December 1999

increased opportunity for women performers and for members of racial and ethnic minorities. Actors' Equity helped spearhead the creation of the National Endowment for the Arts, which has fostered not-for-profit theater in America.

Another note of promise: Employment of dancers, choreographers, musicians, actors, and directors is expected to grow faster than the average for all occupations through the year 2006. Audiences for these talents are likely to grow, predicts the U.S. Department of Labor.

The flip side, of course, is that steady employment is elusive.

The Screen Actors Guild reports that the average income its members earn from acting is less than $5,000 a year. In 1998, first-year dancers earned $543 per week, according to the American Guild of Musical Artists. About half of musicians who are working are employed only part-time.

Official projections and statistics do not tell the whole story, however. There is another way to measure your potential in a performing arts career: Watch trends.

TRENDS

What is happening now gives a clue as to what could happen tomorrow. Trends are not predictions. Trends simply tell us where we appear to be headed. Trend watching—guessing at what will be hot and what will not—has even become a way to earn a living. Why not use trend-watching techniques to investigate your own future in the arts? Here are some suggestions:

Become a clipper. If the arts and entertainment or business sections of your newspaper carry an item on the field you are following, cut it out. Do the same with magazines and professional journals.

Become a skipper. Make your reading time pay off by setting your sights on items that will help you broaden your business knowledge about the arts. Of course you can still read the comics, but train yourself to skip, too.

Become an interpreter. Why rely only on others' observations of what the news means? Draw your own conclusions. This calls for higher-order thinking and reading skills that also will help you in countless ways in your work and personal life. Whatever you read, consider the source. Some sources are more reliable than others, but there is no such thing as a purely objective analysis from anyone. All events are subject to differences in perception. This is why your interpretations are critical.

Become an interviewer. Whenever you have an opportunity to learn about your field of interest from an insider, ask questions. Listen to the answers. Then ask the same questions of other insiders. Compare answers. Again, draw your own conclusions.

Take note, too, of what professional trend watchers are saying about the outlook in performing arts. Should you have faith in their words? No, not as infallible oracles. Consider them one more data source for your files. Read them, as you read this, critically. And have faith in yourself and your own opinions.

OF ZAP AND ZAPPA

The thesaurus is a wonderful beast. In one brief entry in *Doubleday Roget's Thesaurus in Dictionary Form,* an entire doctrine for success in the performing arts can be found:

> zap *Slang n.* push, drive, muscle, vigor, energy, aggressiveness, punch, determination, thrust, vim, strength, vitality, pep, impetus.

Frank Zappa, whose interests ranged from rock to classics, would have added other words to the list: *guts* and *interest span.* In an interview with Laurence Vittes, Zappa had some hard-nosed advice for classical musicians:

> Here's the problem: Most people who have devoted themselves to some sort of artistic endeavor are not good at business. They don't have the guts, the interest span, or the drive. Based on the classical musicians I've met, they'd be eaten alive. They'd probably be better advised to keep their money where they'll get the best return on their dollar. Plan for survival. My advice to people who want to make money from classical music is: Get a real estate license.

Zappa, who never was accused of a tasteful choice of words (or names), nevertheless voices a reality. Those who choose a career in the performing arts will do it for love, not money.

SUCCESS: IT'S YOUR BUSINESS

The performing artists who learn the business end of the arts will have an increased opportunity to find work doing what they love to do. A few schools are beginning to establish courses to lead arts students to better understand business practices and to increase their employability skills. One school, the California Institute of the Arts, has successfully pioneered such a program. The school surveyed alumni to find that 90 percent were doing at least some work in the arts.

Whether the school you choose to attend offers business and career counseling, make it your personal business to learn these marketplace basics. Because it *is* your business. Even the best academic programs, teachers, and mentors cannot guarantee success. Ultimately, you hold your future in your own hands. A performer of the highest calibre, Lily Tomlin, said it best:

"Remember, we're all in this alone."

SOURCES FOR MORE INFORMATION IN THE PERFORMING ARTS

BROCHURES AND DIRECTORIES

The American Music Therapy Association
    8455 Colesville Road, Suite #1000
    Silver Spring, MD 20910
    Website: www.musictherapy.org

The brochure *Music Therapy as a Career* is available and may be acquired by a request that includes a self-addressed, stamped envelope.

Central Opera Service Bulletin
    Metropolitan Opera
    Lincoln Center
    New York, NY 10023

A directory/bulletin, *Career Guide for Young American Singers,* is available from the Met.

Interlochen Center for the Arts
Interlochen, MI 49643

The school provides brochures and related information describing academic and camp programs for arts students.

Music Educators National Conference
1902 Association Drive
Reston, VA 22091

A free copy of *Careers in Music* is available on request.

National Association of Schools of Music
11250 Roger Bacon Drive, Suite 21
Reston, VA 22090

Request their brochure, *Information/National Assn. of Schools of Music,* available at no charge. Or, visit their website, www.arts-accredit.org

National Endowment for the Arts
1100 Pennsylvania Avenue, NW, Room 617
Washington, DC 20506

A booklet, *Guide to the National Endowment for the Arts,* newly revised for the year 2000, is available on request.

BOOKS

Anderson, Stephen. *So, You Wanna Be a Rock Star? How to Create Music, Get Gigs, and Maybe Even Make It Big.* Hillsboro, OR: Beyond Words, 1999.

Bentley, Toni. *Winter Season: A Dancer's Journal.* New York: Random House, 1982.

Bone, Jan. *Opportunities in Film Careers.* Lincolnwood, IL: VGM Career Books, 1998.

Ellis, Roger. *Audition Monologs for Student Actors.* Colorado Springs, CO: Meriwether Publishing, Ltd., 1999.

Everett, Carole J. *The Performing Arts Major's College Guide,* 3rd edition. Indianapolis, IN: Arco MacMillan, 1998.

Foulkes, Richard. *Teach Yourself Theatre.* Lincolnwood, IL: NTC/Contemporary Publishing Group, Inc., 2000.

Gerardi, Robert. *Opportunities in Music Careers.* Lincolnwood, IL: VGM Career Books, 1997.

Greenspon, Jaq. *Careers for Film Buffs & Other Hollywood Types.* Lincolnwood, IL: VGM Career Books, 1998.

Howie, Diana M. *Tight Spots: True-to-Life Monolog Characterizations for Student Actors.* Colorado Springs, CO: Meriwether Publishing, Ltd., 1999.

Johnson, Jeff. *Careers for Music Lovers & Other Tuneful Types.* Lincolnwood, IL: VGM Career Books, 1998.

Kennedy, Joyce Lain. *Joyce Lain Kennedy's Career Book,* 3rd edition. Lincolnwood, IL: VGM Career Books, 1996.

London, Mel. *Getting Into Film.* New York: Ballantine Books, 1986.

Lydon, Michael. *How to Succeed in Show Business by Really Trying.* New York: Dodd Mead, 1985.

MacLeod, Joseph. *Actor's Right to Act.* Amherst, NY: Prometheus, 1981.

Mayfield, Katherine. *The Young Person's Guide to a Stage or Screen Career.* New York. Watson-Guptill Publications, 1998

Peterson's Scholarships for Study in the USA & Canada, 3rd edition. Princeton, NJ: Peterson's, 1998.

Peterson's Professional Degree Programs in the Visual & Performing Arts, 2000 Edition. Princeton, NJ: Peterson's, 1997.

Silver, Fred. *How to Audition for the Musical Theatre.* New York: Market Press, 1985.

Vilga, Edward. *Acting Now: Conversations on Craft and Career.* Piscataway, NJ: Rutgers University Press, 1997.

ASSOCIATIONS, ORGANIZATIONS, UNIONS

Dance

American Dance Guild
570 Seventh Avenue, 20th Floor
New York, NY 10018

American Dance Therapy Association
2000 Century Plaza, Suite 230
Columbia, MD 21004

Dance Educators of America
P.O. Box 509
Oceanside, NY 11572

National Association for Schools of Dance, Art, Music, and
Theatre
11250 Roger Bacon Drive, Suite 21
Reston, VA 22090

National Dance Association
1900 Association Drive
Reston, VA 22091

National Research Centers for Arts in Education
New York University, Director of Dance
35 West Fourth Street, Room 615
New York, NY 10003

National Research Centers for Arts in Education
University of Illinois, Director of Dance
500 South Goodwin Avenue
Urbana, IL 61801

Theater, Film

Actors' Equity Association
165 West 46th Street
New York, NY 10036

American Federation of Television and Radio Artists
   1350 Avenue of the Americas
   New York, NY 10019

American Theatre Association
   1010 Wisconsin Avenue NW
   Washington, DC 20007

Hispanic Institute for the Performing Arts
   1629 K Street NW, Suite 800
   Washington, DC 20006

League of Professional Theatre Training Programs
   1860 Broadway, Suite 1515
   New York, NY 10023

Performing and Visual Arts Society
   P.O. Box 102
   Kinnelon, NJ 07405

Screen Actors Guild
   7750 Sunset Boulevard
   Los Angeles, CA 90046

Music

American Composers Alliance
   170 West 74th Street
   New York, NY 10023

American Guild of Music Artists
  1841 Broadway
  New York, NY 10023

American Music Conference
  1000 Skokie Boulevard
  Wilmette, IL 60091

American Society of Music Copyists
  Box 41 Radio City Station
  New York, NY 10101

American Symphony Orchestra League
  633 E Street NW
  Washington, DC 20004

Music Educators National Conference
  1902 Association Drive
  Reston, VA 22091

National Association of Schools of Music
  11250 Roger Bacon Drive, Suite 21
  Reston, VA 22090

National Orchestra Association
  111 W. 57th Street, Suite 1400
  New York, NY 10019

APPENDIX B

BIBLIOGRAPHY

Angel, Johnny. "Cattle Call: Actors Are Clawing Their Way Through Casting Offices for the Chance to Become the Next Famous Face." *New Times,* September 23, 1999.

Canadian Actors Equity Website. "CAEA Auditions." www.cace.com. January 3, 2000.

Gere, David. "The New Era in Dance." *Performing Arts, February 1989, 25–29.*

Guinto, Liesl. "Artist's Dilemma: Staying Happy and Solvent Until the Big Break Happens." *Los Angeles Times,* August 1, 1999.

Haithman, Diane. "As American as Chinese Strudel." *Times/ Calendar,* November 26, 1999, 46.

Isenberg, Barbara. "Moved to Make the Connection." *Times/ Calendar,* November 26, 1999, 8.

Lewis, Judith. "How Andy Prieboy Created *White Trash." L.A. Weekly.* December 3, 1999.

McQuilkin, Terry, "Randall Behr." *Los Angeles Times,* April 22, 1989.

Parachini, Allan. "Artists' Outlook: An Overcrowded Landscape." *Los Angeles Times,* November 11, 1989.

Sadownick, Douglas. "Choreographer in the Spotlight." *Times/Calendar,* April 23, 1989, 61.

Screen Actors Guild Website. "SAG-Sponsored Bill Protecting Child Performers Signed Into Law." November 29, 1999. www.sag.com

Segal, Lewis. "Russian Star Ruzimatov's Range Ends in Artistic High." *Los Angeles Times,* November 13, 1999.

Sills, Beverly. "Introduction." *Central Opera Service Career Guide for Young American Singers.* Vol. 25, No. 4.

Swed, Mark. "The Dalai Lama's View." *Times/Calendar,* September 19, 1999.

Vaughn, Susan. "If They Didn't Love Their Jobs, They'd Be Singing the Blues." *Los Angeles Times,* August 16, 1999.

Vittes, Laurence. "Frank Zappa Has a Tip for Serious Musicians." *Reader,* October 13, 1989, 6–7.